WARRIOR • 155

ANZAC INFANTRYMAN 1914–15

From New Guinea to Gallipoli

IAN SUMNER ILLUSTRATED BY GRAHAM TURNER

Series editor Marcus Cowper

First published in Great Britain in 2011 by Osprey Publishing
Midland House, West Way, Botley, Oxford OX2 0PH, UK
44-02 23rd St, Suite 219, Long Island City, NY 11101, USA
E-mail: info@ospreypublishing.com

© 2011 Osprey Publishing Ltd.

All rights reserved. Apart from any fair dealing for the purpose of private study, research, criticism or review, as permitted under the Copyright, Designs and Patents Act, 1988, no part of this publication may be reproduced, stored in a retrieval system, or transmitted in any form or by any means, electronic, electrical, chemical, mechanical, optical, photocopying, recording or otherwise, without the prior written permission of the copyright owner. Enquiries should be addressed to the Publishers.

A CIP catalogue record for this book is available from the British Library.

ISBN: 978 1 84908 328 7

E-book ISBN: 978 1 84908 329 4

Editorial by Ilios Publishing Ltd, Oxford, UK (www.iliospublishing.com)
Page layout by: Mark Holt
Index by Margaret Vaudrey
Typeset in Sabon and Myriad Pro
Originated by PDQ Media
Printed in China through Worldprint Ltd

11 12 13 14 10 9 8 7 6 5 4 3 2 1

www.ospreypublishing.com

ACKNOWLEDGEMENTS

My thanks must, as ever, go to my wife for all her assistance. Thanks also to the staffs of the Special Collections department of the Brotherton Library at Leeds University and the Alexander Turnbull Library, Wellington, New Zealand. Photographs from the Liddle Collection are reproduced with the permission of the Brotherton Collection, Leeds University Library.

ARTIST'S NOTE

Readers may care to note that the original paintings from which the colour plates in this book were prepared are available for private sale.
All reproduction copyright whatsoever is retained by the Publishers.
All enquiries should be addressed to:

Graham Turner
PO Box 568
Aylesbury
HP17 8ZX

www.studio88.co.uk

The Publishers regret that they can enter into no correspondence upon this matter.

THE WOODLAND TRUST

Osprey Publishing are supporting the Woodland Trust, the UK's leading woodland conservation charity, by funding the dedication of trees.

CONTENTS

INTRODUCTION	4
CHRONOLOGY	6
RECRUITMENT	10
TRAINING	17
UNIFORM AND EQUIPMENT	23
STRAIGHT INTO ACTION	31
ON THE BEACHHEAD	43
OUT OF ACTION	51
AWAY FROM THE FRONT	56
ANZAC	61
MUSEUMS AND RE-ENACTMENT	62
FURTHER READING	63
INDEX	64

ANZAC INFANTRYMAN 1914–15

INTRODUCTION

When the Commonwealth of Australia was created in 1901 it took over responsibility for defence matters from the six former crown colonies. The military and naval units of the individual colonies were transferred to the new commonwealth and merged into a single organization with a standardized set of regulations. In peacetime, enlistment was voluntary; but the 1904 Defence Act permitted the governor general to call up all males between the ages of 16 and 60 for service within Australia in time of war.

The Australian Government was wary of the increasing power of Japan and the German Pacific colonies of Samoa and New Guinea, and in 1908 introduced a new bill to permit peacetime conscription. The following year Prime Minister Alfred Deakin invited Field Marshal Viscount Kitchener to visit Australia and advise on the best means of the country equipping itself with a land defence. Kitchener recommended that Australia needed a military force of 80,000 men, as well as a military college and a staff corps.

Only conscription could produce the number of men required, and in 1910 the new defence act became law. Males between the ages of 12 and 18 became cadets. Boys of 12 years and over were liable for a minimum of 90 hours of military training each year, increasing to 96 hours at age 14. At 18 the cadets transferred to an active battalion. Here, for the next seven years, they would undertake the equivalent of 16 days of training a year (including eight served at an annual camp). With each class reckoned to produce around 17,000 men, by 1914 the Army would be around 45,000 strong. The old militia system was to be phased out, with only officers and NCOs allowed to transfer to the new force.

Founded in June 1911, the Royal Military College at Duntroon (New South Wales) was open to any suitable candidate between the ages of 16 and 19. Candidates were admitted on a pro-rata basis in line with the population of each state and also included ten New Zealand cadets a year. By 1914, the Australian Army was made up principally of soldiers aged between 19 and 21, and these young men went on to form the nucleus of the Australian Imperial Force (AIF).

On leaving Australia, Lord Kitchener carried on to New Zealand, where he recommended a similar scheme. From the ages of 14 to 18, boys were to serve in the senior cadets, before transferring to the Territorial regiments for a further seven years. The annual Territorial commitment for each man consisted of 31 drill parades, 12 half-day parades and a seven-day camp. This, it was estimated, would produce an army of two infantry divisions and four mounted-rifle brigades, a total of around 30,000 men, with an additional 59,000 reserves.

Kitchener's plans dealt only with national defence, paying little attention to the question of raising forces for operations outside Australasia. Britain and its self-governing dominions had first discussed this issue at the Colonial Conference of 1902. The dominions at that time were each making a financial contribution towards their wider defence. Britain suggested that each should

A cheerful-looking Trooper Allan Huthwaite of 1st Light Horse is photographed at No. 1 Outpost. He is apparently using the copious pockets of his tunic to great advantage. A drover in civilian life, Huthwaite hailed from Goulborn (New South Wales), and died of his wounds in 1917. (E. N. Merrington Collection, Turnbull Library)

instead establish a small expeditionary force, which might also be capable of acting as an Imperial reserve in the event of an emergency. However, the dominions deemed this too aggressive a step and rejected the proposal.

The crisis that blew up in Europe following the assassination of Archduke Franz Ferdinand in July 1914 caused a rapid change of heart. On 30 July, New Zealand offered Britain an expeditionary force of 6,000 troops should the situation require it. Australia was in the throes of a federal election campaign and found it impossible to respond immediately. But Brigadier William Bridges (Inspector-General of the Australian Army and the future commander of the AIF) quickly took charge of the situation. Acting on his own initiative, Bridges sent a warning order to the forces in each state; so when Australia finally took the decision to offer troops on 2 August, the authorities were already prepared.

But how many men should the country send? In the wake of the Kitchener reforms, the Australian and New Zealand governments had already met to discuss the possibility of forming a joint division, to comprise 12,000 Australians and 6,000 New Zealanders. With New Zealand now offering 6,000 men, Australia had to send at least 12,000. But news that Canada was about to volunteer as many as 30,000 troops encouraged Australian Prime Minister Sir Joseph Cook to commit a larger force. On 3 August he sent an offer of 20,000 men to London, and three days later Britain accepted it.

CHRONOLOGY

1914

5 August	Recruitment begins for the AIF – troops offered to Britain in time of war.
6 August	Australian Naval and Military Expeditionary Force (ANMEF) forms up.
14 August	ANMEF leaves Australia for islands of Yap, Nauru and New Britain.
15 August	ANMEF leaves New Zealand for Samoa.
29 August	Samoa occupied without resistance.
11 September	ANMEF arrives off Rabaul, New Britain.
17 September	German colony of New Guinea surrenders.
1 November	First ships carrying AIF leave Australia.
3 December	AIF begins disembarkation in Egypt.
21 December	Major-General Birdwood takes command of Australian & New Zealand Army Corps (ANZAC).

1915

25 January	New Zealand Infantry Brigade ordered to Suez Canal.
1 February	Advance parties of 4th Australian Infantry Brigade arrive at Zeitoun.
3 February	Turkish troops attack Suez Canal; New Zealanders engaged.
26 February	New Zealand Infantry Brigade returns from Suez Canal.
1 April	ANZAC formations ordered to Gallipoli.
9 April	New Zealand and Australian Division, less mounted units, entrains for Alexandria.
10 April	First transports leave for Mudros.
25 April	ANZAC lands at Anzac Cove – the 3rd Australian Infantry Brigade is first ashore at dawn.
26 April	Turkish counter-attacks beaten off at Anzac.
27 April	Heavy attack against centre and Walker's Ridge beaten off at 0930hrs.
28 April	Portsmouth and Chatham Battalions (Royal Marine Brigade) arrive at 1800hrs.
29 April	Heavy Turkish attacks all along Anzac line; a naval brigade (Nelson and Deal Battalions) arrives that night as reinforcement.
2 May	Canterbury Battalion destroys Turkish observation post at Lala Baba.
2–3 May	Otago Battalion attack on Baby 700 fails.
3 May	Turkish warship fires on transports anchored offshore.
4 May	Turks beat off Australian raid on Gaba Tepe.
5–6 May	New Zealand Infantry Brigade and 2nd Australian Brigade leave for Cape Helles.
6 May	Combined French, British and Colonial Forces launch attack on Krithia.
8 May	New Zealand Infantry Brigade and 2nd Australian Brigade defeated at Krithia.

10 May	Australians at head of Monash Gully attack Turks but later withdraw.
12 May	New Zealand Mounted Rifles Brigade arrives at Anzac to fight as infantry; Australian light-horse regiments arrive at Anzac.
14 May	Queenslanders launch sortie from Quinn's Post, the most advanced position on the Anzac line.
16 May	A 6in. howitzer with RMLI crew arrives in support.
17 May	2nd Australian Infantry Brigade returns from Helles; three guns (2nd Battery, New Zealand Field Artillery) hauled up to Plugge's Plateau.
18 May	Heavy Turkish attacks; German Taube flies over Anzac.
19 May	Turkish attack at Anzac defeated; New Zealand Infantry Brigade returns from Helles.
20 May	Otago Mounted Rifles arrive at Anzac to fight as infantry; Turks make first request for armistice.
24 May	Armistice day to bury dead.
28 May	Turks fire mine by night in front of Quinn's Post; Canterbury Mounted Rifles take Old No. 3 Post.
29 May	Turks attack Quinn's Post – Major Quinn killed.
31 May	Turkish blockhouse in front of Quinn's Post is blown up; Mounted Rifles forced from Old No. 3 Post.
4 June	Canterbury Battalion launch night raid from Quinn's Post.
5 June	Sortie against German Officers' Trench opposite Courtney's Post.
7–8 June	Night sortie from Quinn's Post.
10 June	Scouting parties of New Zealand Mounted Rifles driven back to No. 2 Post.
12 June	4.5in. howitzer taken from Howitzer Gully up to Plugge's Plateau.
29–30 June	Last Turkish attack at Anzac fails.
31 July	200 men of the 11th West Australian Battalion take Turkish trenches opposite Tasmania Post.

3 August	The 13th (New Army) Division arrives at Anzac.
6–7 August	Australians attack at Lone Pine, Quinn's Post and Russell's Top; New Zealand Mounted Rifles retake Old No. 3 Post, take Table Top and Bauchop's Hill; Left Covering Force (Travers' 40th Brigade) takes Damakjelik Bair.
7 August	Rhododendron Spur in New Zealand hands; attack by Auckland Battalion fails.
8 August	Wellington Battalion captures Chunuk Bair; reinforced during day by Auckland Mounted Rifles; relieved that night by Otago Battalion and Wellington Mounted Rifles.
9 August	New Zealanders hold Chunuk Bair; relieved that night by New Army troops.
10 August	Turkish counter-attack drives New Army troops from Chunuk Bair.
21 August	First attack on Hill 60.
27 August	Battle for Hill 60 renewed.
28 August	New Zealanders consolidate hold on Hill 60.
11 September	Lord Kitchener asks Sir Ian Hamilton for cost of evacuation; 'evacuation unthinkable' is his reply.
Mid-September	First batch of troops withdrawn to Sarpi Rest Camp (Lemnos).
2 November	4th Australian Infantry Brigade returns from Sarpi Rest Camp.
10 November	New Zealand Mounted Rifles return from Mudros Rest Camp.
13 November	Kitchener visits Anzac.
24 November	Period of silence ordered and lasts 72 hours.
26 November	Lieutenant-General Birdwood takes overall command on peninsula; Godley, promoted to the rank of lieutenant-general, takes command of the ANZAC.
27–28 November	The 'Great Blizzard' begins.
8 December	Lieutenant-General Birdwood orders evacuation of Anzac and Suvla.
10–11 December	All sick, wounded, surplus troops, vehicles and valuable stores are removed from Anzac Cove.

12 December	Formation of winter rest camp on Imbros announced at Anzac; surplus guns removed.
15 December	Detailed orders issued for evacuation.
19 December	Last night of evacuation at Anzac and Suvla.
20 December	Evacuation of Anzac and Suvla complete by daylight; troops disembark at Lemnos.

RECRUITMENT

Despite their earlier discussions, the Australian and New Zealand governments had given no real thought to the exact composition of any future joint force. 'How did the British War Office want the force to be organized?' they now asked. As a complete division? Or as a series of brigade-sized formations? The Australians naturally wanted their men to serve together. But aware that Britain held no high opinion of Australian abilities, they feared she would prefer smaller formations serving separately within larger British ones. And this was just what happened. The British requested a force consisting of three separate brigades – two of infantry and one of light horse, plus supporting field artillery.

The Australian and New Zealand staffs had first to decide whether they wished to use existing battalions or raise new units from scratch. So many men were needed in so short a time that Australia chose the second option. The Kitchener reforms had yet to take full effect, and the cadre of experienced men was too small to employ existing battalions. Even before Australia had made its formal offer of troops, men were coming forward to enlist in the new AIF. A small staff was set up at Victoria Barracks in Melbourne to register their names. As far as possible, preference would go to men aged 20 or over who had already received military training. Half of these would be drawn from the post-Kitchener Army; the other half must either have served under the old militia system or during the Second Boer War. The most experienced men, those currently serving as warrant officers and NCOs, were appointed as regimental sergeant majors and/or quartermaster sergeants.

Each unit was connected with a particular Australian state. In the case of specialist arms such as the artillery, the engineers and the medical corps, this principle was later abandoned; but it continued to hold good for the infantry and light horse until the end of the war. New South Wales and Victoria each raised a brigade of four battalions, while the less populous states of Queensland, South Australia, Western Australia and Tasmania raised a brigade between them. Many of the recruits for the light horse were raised from Queensland cattle-farming districts, where men were used to handling horses. And they had to be exceptionally competent, for the standards of horsemanship required to gain acceptance were very high indeed.

By the end of 1914 as many as 53,000 men had volunteered. Extra brigades – of both infantry and light horse – were formed, and Britain gratefully accepted their services. A second contingent – made up of the Australian 4th Infantry Brigade, some 10,500 strong, plus a further 2,000 New Zealanders – sailed in late December 1914. Further reinforcements followed at a rate of 3,200 men a month.

A group of new recruits are pictured at Broadmeadows Camp, on the outskirts of Melbourne (Victoria). Although it is December 1914, these men are still dressed in a mixture of pre-war uniform and civilian clothing. (Liddle Collection)

The flood of volunteers allowed individual battalions to adopt specific recruiting areas and form up using men from the same region. So, for example, 2nd Battalion drew on the Maitland and Newcastle coalfields in New South Wales, while 5th and 6th Battalions recruited in Melbourne. Meanwhile, 7th and 8th Battalions looked to the goldfields of Victoria – 7th Battalion to Bendigo and 8th Battalion to Ballarat.

By April 1915 contemporary newspapers reported that some 12,000 shearers and station hands had enlisted, as well as 1,000 bank clerks. In New South Wales, 164 students at the state agricultural college enlisted together, as did 140 policemen. Rejected in one state, many men simply travelled elsewhere to enlist. One determined volunteer rode 460 miles (740km) to a railway station, then travelled on by train to join the light horse at Adelaide. Here too the ranks were full, so he sailed to Hobart, and finally enlisted in Sydney.

In contrast, New Zealand built its expeditionary force around its existing military structure, and its men therefore retained their old regimental badges. Pre-war planners had already set the size of any potential expeditionary force. Geared to the country's total manpower, this figure determined the rate at which reinforcements would later be trained and supplied. Each of the four military districts – Auckland, Canterbury, Otago and Wellington – would provide sufficient men to create an infantry battalion and a mounted rifles regiment. Meanwhile, each of the four companies making up a battalion would be drawn from a single Territorial regiment. For example, the four companies comprising the Wellington Battalion were raised from volunteers from the 7th Wellington West Coast, 9th Hawke's Bay, 11th Taranaki Rifles and 17th Ruahine Regiments respectively. The same principle applied to the Mounted Rifles – each of their squadrons would be drawn from a single Territorial cavalry regiment.

This placed a disproportionate burden on some sparsely populated rural areas, particularly in the Otago and Canterbury districts, which lacked the manpower to provide the number of replacements required. By the end

With a band leading the way, 6th Reinforcements march to Lambton Quay, Wellington, for embarkation. The men left New Zealand on 14 August 1915 aboard the transports *Wilochra* and *Tofua*, and reached Suez on 19 September. They were probably the last New Zealand reinforcements to reach Gallipoli before the troops withdrew. (John Dickie Collection, Turnbull Library)

of the campaign the system was beginning to break down under the weight of casualties, and replacements were sent where they were most needed rather than to their own local unit.

Imperial policy opposed the use of native peoples in a war between Europeans. But opinions began to change with the performance of Indian troops in Egypt and France, and the first Native Contingent arrived in Egypt in March as part of 3rd Reinforcements. Former member of parliament Te Rangi Hiroa (Peter Buck) served as medical officer in the Native Contingent and argued that his men should be given the chance to see combat: 'Our ancestors were a warlike people … the members of this war party would be ashamed to face their people at the conclusion of the war if they were to be confined entirely to garrison duty and not be given an opportunity of proving their mettle at the front.'

Despite his plea, the Maori were immediately dispatched to Malta as garrison troops. Not everyone was impressed: the commanding officer of the Wellington Regiment thought them 'mostly big hulking gone-in-the-knees walking men… They look soft.' The Maori were eventually sent to Gallipoli in early July and attached to the Mounted Rifles Brigade as pioneers. A total of 50 men of the Native Contingent would be killed on the peninsula.

Queenslander Wilbraham Fowler, a bank clerk serving in 15th Battalion, felt it his 'bounden duty as a single man' to volunteer. He felt obliged to uphold 'the glorious traditions and the everlasting supremacy of the good old British Empire'. Meanwhile, Private C. L. Comyns, of the Wellington Battalion, went to sleep at Trentham Camp thinking of himself as 'a one-day-old British soldier'. The contemporary Australian education system certainly placed great store on the link between Britain and its dominions, on the virtues of patriotism, and the glory of empire. However, many volunteers may have responded to a more personal motivation; almost one quarter of those who enlisted were British born (and many more had British-born parents).

Others were moved by a spirit of adventure. Like Bill Harney of 25th Battalion, later a well-known writer, they just wanted to be 'in it' before the war ended: 'I was dead scared when I went to join up – scared it would be all over before I got there!' Edward Brew was under age when he tried to join up in Melbourne, and his parents reclaimed him. But the next day he slipped out of his house again, travelled to Sydney, and successfully entered the ranks of 2nd Battalion. Another under-age soldier was Tasmanian Alec Campbell, who joined up at 16 and arrived at Gallipoli in November 1915. 'I must have lied about my age,' he confessed artlessly in an interview in 1997. 'It was a bit of an adventure at that age – Egypt was a fairy land – but I suppose we had some idea of protecting Australia and England.' Campbell was the last Gallipoli veteran to die, aged 103, in 2002.

Potential volunteers faced a strict medical examination. Every man had to be a minimum of 5ft 6in. (168cm) tall, with a chest measurement of 34in. (86cm). Those slighter in build were allowed to enlist as artillery drivers. Outsiders would later comment favourably on Australian troops, remarking how tall and well-built they appeared, particularly in comparison with their counterparts in British Territorial and 'Pals' battalions. But the Australian recruiters had the benefit of much greater discretion; the large number of volunteers and the limited number of places available allowed them to pick only those they saw as the best.

Those who were turned away experienced palpable distress. One medical officer recalled: 'Many of them have thrown up good jobs, and have travelled hundreds of miles. They have been feted as heroes before leaving, and would rather die than go back rejected. Some I have to refuse, and they plead with me and almost break down – in fact some do go away, poor chaps, gulping down their feelings and with tears of disappointment in their eyes.' But standards changed as the casualty lists mounted, and men initially rejected for relatively minor reasons – dental problems, for example – were later accepted.

1st Division provides a good example of the mix of volunteers who passed muster. Its initial complement included 2,263 young trainee soldiers and 1,555 older militiamen. A further 2,460 men had seen some service in the militia, 1,308 were former regulars in the British Army and 1,009 had served in the British Territorial Force. This left as many as 6,098 (just over 40 per cent) who had no military experience at all.

The new recruits marched to the docks along streets crowded with family and well-wishers. As the newspapers put it, they were 'Off On The Great Adventure'. Signaller Robert Kenny of 4th Battalion wrote:

> When we left Sydney nobody knew we were going... How it leaked out ... I don't know but soon people came flocking from everywhere. The police cordon could hardly keep back the women bent on giving father or brother a parting kiss. We were reminded before leaving camp that breaking ranks or any breach of discipline would be severely dealt with; and every man stood like a statue. But I shall not forget the tear-dimmed eyes of the women and girls that I saw on the morning I left Sydney.

Watching the milling crowds at Melbourne from the deck of the transport *Clan Macgillivray*, Lieutenant Burford Sampson of 15th Battalion confided in his diary, 'I hate farewells at boat or train'. He was glad to see that 'there was not a living soul on the pier I knew'.

1st Division left Australia on 1 November, reaching Cairo on 4 December. But it was not the first Antipodean force to take the field. At the beginning of the conflict, Britain had asked Australia and New Zealand to perform 'a great and urgent Imperial service', by capturing the German colonies of New Guinea and Samoa. Both housed powerful radio stations that could be used to direct German commerce raiders onto Allied shipping, and both were capable of

The transport SS *Geelong* slips her moorings at Hobart in front of a large crowd of well-wishers. On board was the first Tasmanian contingent to join the AIF, part of 9th Field Battery. (Liddle Collection)

providing shelter for those same raiders. Australia and New Zealand were quick to answer the call. The Australian Military and Naval Expeditionary Force, consisting of a single battalion raised in New South Wales and a six-company-strong naval brigade drawn from four of the states, set sail for New Guinea, taking the country with minimal casualties. As for Samoa, the New Zealand Government sent five companies from one of its Territorial regiments – the 5th Wellington – to secure the islands.

News that the Anzac divisions were in action in the Dardanelles acted as a spur to recruitment during the early summer of 1915. In the first four months of that year 33,758 men volunteered; in the next four months another 85,320 joined them. 'I do not think that I was ever a great man for heroics', confessed one Victorian recruit, 'yet I go to join in it, believing that the only hope for the salvation of the world is a speedy victory for the Allies.' Extra camps were needed to accommodate the new men, and at Ballarat Show Grounds (Victoria) the recruits slept on boards laid down in the animal pens.

Sufficient men were recruited to form three new brigades – 5th, 6th and 7th – which were all sent to Egypt as 2nd Australian Division in August 1915. Australia also complied with a British request to provide a battery of howitzers

A — **PRIVATES, AUSTRALIAN NAVAL AND MILITARY EXPEDITIONARY FORCE, AUSTRALIA 1914**

By comparison with the old militia, the size of the post-1912 Army was immense. The Government sought to reduce costs by providing a simple uniform that was easy to manufacture in large quantities. Accordingly, a much more utilitarian set of garments replaced the colourful full-dress uniforms of the militia.

The single battalion that formed the Army component of the Australian Naval and Military Expeditionary Force (ANMEF) wore the new uniform, following the 1912 regulations. For other ranks, the uniform consisted of a bush hat with the left side turned up, bearing the Australian Military Forces 'sunburst' badge, and with a puggaree coloured by arm of service; a woollen 'military shirt', with a short tab closure with brass buttons, and buttoned cuffs; and dismounted-pattern breeches, tucked into puttees. Their equipment was the 1908 webbing set. Officers and senior NCOs were permitted to retain a British-style jacket – by 1914 officers were wearing their jackets with an open neck and a collar and tie; the NCOs, however, retained a closed collar.

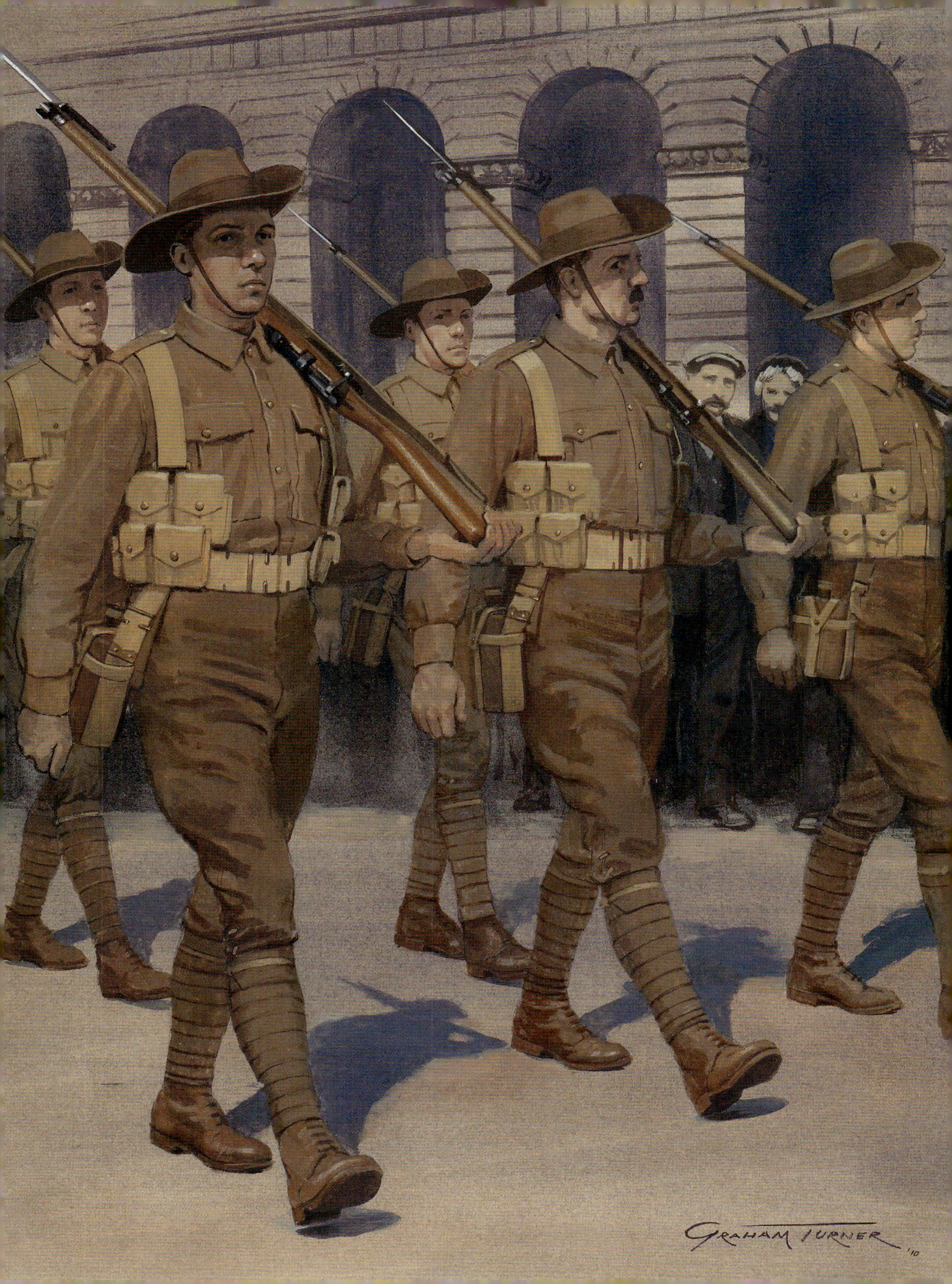
GRAHAM TURNER
'10

for service in Turkey (although administrative problems prevented the unit from reaching Egypt until early September), and offered a 'mining corps' of 1,000 men – a proposal London accepted with alacrity. One civilian was puzzled by the scene as the new division marched away. They set off 'singing, shouting and cheering', he reported. 'Yet every day they see thousands of their comrades walking around the streets wounded.'

The AIF and the New Zealand Expeditionary Force were combined into a single formation, named the Australian and New Zealand Army Corps. The new corps consisted of one wholly Australian division, a mixed New Zealand and Australian division (made up of New Zealand infantry and a brigade of Australian light horse), a brigade of New Zealand Mounted Rifles and a further brigade of Australian light horse. Combining Australian and New Zealand troops in this way seemed appropriate to the British, given that the two countries were neighbours. But geographical proximity did not necessarily mean that Australians and New Zealanders saw eye to eye. War correspondent C. E. W. Bean, author of *The Official History of Australia in the War of 1914–1918*, contrasted the two peoples. For Bean, the Australians 'were easily the most noticeable and the most frequent offenders… I think we have to admit that our force contains more bad hats than the others; and I also think that the average Australian is certainly a harder liver.' In contrast, he judged the New Zealanders colourless, without the 'extraordinarily good points' displayed by his own countrymen.

Trooper Claude Pocock, of the Canterbury Mounted Rifles, more than returned the animus: 'the Australian, and more especially the town-bred man, is a skiting bumptious fool who thinks nobody knows anything but himself. If we meet or see them in a restaurant or anywhere in town there is generally a row of some kind.'

Yet, despite this mutual antagonism, the new Australian and New Zealand Army Corps quickly began to develop a common identity. This was helped by a simple administrative decision. Looking for an abbreviated form of the name to put on a stamp for official documents, someone hit on A&NZAC. And, from this, it was a simple matter to shorten the name once again – this time to 'Anzac'.

The New Zealanders land in Apia, Samoa, 27 August 1914. Standing in the stern of the nearest boat is the battalion commander, Lieutenant-Colonel (later Brigadier-General) Harry Fulton. The New Zealanders met with no resistance on Samoa; however, in New Guinea, the Australians had several skirmishes with local troops. (Hackworth Collection, Turnbull Library)

TRAINING

Those lucky enough to be accepted for service were gathered together in camps: in Australia, for example, Blackboy Hill (Western Australia), Brighton (Tasmania), Broadmeadows (Victoria), Enoggera (Queensland), Liverpool (New South Wales) and Morphetville (South Australia); and in New Zealand, Alexandra Park (Auckland), Awapuni Racecourse (Wellington), Addington Park (Christchurch) and Tahuna Park (Otago). The first contingent of troops spent six weeks in camp, but little could be done in the way of training. Most of their time was spent in drill, getting them accustomed to the word of command. Many of the new recruits – such as those who worked on farms – were already used to living under canvas. For these men, thought Trooper Clutha McKenzie of the Wellington Mounted Rifles, military life compared favourably with civilian. 'For most of them,' he observed, 'these were lazy holidays after the hard life of the bush and the sheep-runs.' Others thought differently. Private H. W. Cavell of 2nd Battalion remembered his first night in camp, 'lying on the cement floor of the Randwick grandstand, trousers folded around boots for a pillow, one blanket and many a shiver, while a terrific southerly buster drove the rain in clouds of spray over all who were not fortunate enough to be at the back.'

Generally, indiscipline was rare. No one wished to be discharged and miss out on the adventure to come. But opportunities were taken to weed out those who were judged unsuitable. At Blackboy Hill, one battalion was paraded to witness the discharge of a dozen men who had absented themselves after receiving their pay. These unfortunates were stripped of their uniforms, dressed in plain dungarees and marched out of the battalion lines.

All NCOs were supposed to have previous military experience, but this was not always apparent to their men. Private Arthur Currey, later of the New Zealand Field Artillery, was less than impressed by his NCOs:

> coming from different parts of NZ, [they] tried to show off their good points by shouting loud and long at their men; this used to grate on the ears, especially when we were doing our best... Some of them could not name off the part of their gun without the aid of their handbook. When instructing their men they would bluff their way through by standing off and shouting a lot of quick commands at new men and then bully their men because they had made no progress.

One sergeant from 13th Battalion was reduced to making this plaintive request: 'I'm supposed to give you chaps an hour's fixing and unfixing. Does anyone know anything about it?' Yet another battalion was asked: 'Is there anyone here who would like to be a sergeant?'

Some of the new recruits found military life something of a shock. Ellis Silas, a Perth artist serving as a signaller in 16th Battalion, was worried about the approaching sea journey: 'How will I stand being cooped up with these rough men in such a confined space?' he wondered. 'There are 3,000 of us on board; nowhere quiet where I can go away to think.' The unworldly Silas was later left behind on a route march by his squad whilst he stood marvelling at a sunset, and provoked gales of laughter when he asked for his tea in a china cup instead of a tin mug. Another man confided disapprovingly that 'the moral tone of the mess ... [was] a little lower than a shearing shed'.

The New Zealand contingents, and those from the eastern states of Australia, assembled in King George Sound, off the port of Albany (Western Australia),

Opportunities for keeping fit during the voyage across the Indian Ocean were limited. Here, on board the transport *Omrah*, the officers of 9th Battalion do some early morning exercises – including, from left to right, Lieutenant Haymen, Major Robertson, Lieutenant Hinton, Lieutenant Chapman, Lieutenant Ross, Captain Butler (the battalion Medical Officer) and 2nd Lieutenant Pattison. (E. N. Merrington Collection, Turnbull Library)

where they met up with their Western Australian comrades. Then on 1 November the convoy sailed for Europe. British fears of German commerce raiders were quickly realized when the convoy was threatened by the German light cruiser SMS *Emden*, which had been in Far Eastern waters when war broke out. An engagement took place off the Cocos Islands, and the German ship was forced aground by one of the convoy escorts, HMAS *Sydney*.

Much cheered by this Australian victory, the convoy carried on to Colombo and thence to Aden. Aden failed to impress at least one soldier, who found it lacking the charm of Albany and Colombo. In theory at least, only officers were allowed to leave a ship when it was in port. But some men still managed to make their way ashore, with predictable results. Australian C. E. W. Bean sought to highlight the New Zealand miscreants, having spotted 'numbers of [New Zealanders] laid out in all directions on the landing stage.' He laid the blame on the lack of drink on board their transports. 'They have only dry canteens,' he reported, 'and … are liable to break out at every port they come to.'

The crowded transports provided little space for instruction, and much of the journey passed in forced inactivity. For those accustomed to the better things of life, the food on board ship was a great disappointment. Ship's newspapers allowed the men to vent their frustration, and one paper reported the following conversation between an officer and a private: 'Orderly Officer: "Any complaints men?" Private: "Yessir, taste this, Sir." Officer: "H'm, rather thin and greasy, otherwise not bad soup!" Private: "Yessir, that is what we thought, but the Cook says it's tea".' When another orderly officer asked if there were any complaints he was hit 'fair in the face' by a hunk of old cheese.

Each recruit received one shilling a day to spend at the ship's canteen, but the money did not go far. The canteens were run by private contractors, and complaints about overcharging were soon rife. Even when the Australian and New Zealand governments stepped in to take over, things were no better. Most items were still overpriced and sold out quickly, and little attempt was made to replenish stocks, even at the ports of call. This gave crewmen on the transports the opportunity to step in and fill the void; they could make good money by selling food and drink. On one transport, 'the Butcher sold iced lemon water and made not less than 10/- [ten shillings] per night. The Bakers made a pile with little rock cakes and buns at one penny each.'

The Australian camp at Mena. Behind the ridge in the foreground are the Sphinx and the Pyramids. The Australians found few facilities in the camp when they arrived. However, by the time this photograph was taken, there was a mess hall, cinema and boxing ring. (Liddle Collection)

The Anzacs thought they were heading for Britain, but their destination changed while they were still at sea. The original plan had been to house the troops on Salisbury Plain, but it came to nothing when accommodation could not be made ready in time. Rather than billet the Anzacs in tents through the rigours of an English winter, it was decided to send them to Egypt instead. This was a move with two perceived advantages: the presence of the Anzacs would strengthen the Imperial garrison, so helping to secure the Suez Canal against Turkish attack; and at the same time training could continue in warm weather.

The Anzacs arrived in Egypt at the beginning of December 1914, and three Australian brigade training areas were quickly organized. They were situated in the shadow of the Pyramids, near the village of Mena – 'and what a hole it is', complained one soldier. Carl Janssen, of 5th Battalion, agreed. 'It is sand and more sand', he recorded, 'and we drill in sand up to our ankles and march in sand and eat sand but it is decidedly cleaner than Broadmeadows' dust.' The New Zealanders went to Zeitoun, near Heliopolis, about six miles (9.7km) from Cairo. Private Peter Thompson, of the Otago Battalion, was equally unimpressed. 'Great Scott! What a place!' he wrote. 'Sand, sand, sand everywhere. We are camped in the Sahara Desert.'

Commanders were told to devise training schemes for their men. The Corps was expected to re-embark for France almost immediately, so little time

The New Zealand camp at Zeitoun, complete with its drug store and bookstall. (W. W. Martin Collection, Turnbull Library)

had been allowed for training in the initial plans. One month was allocated for training at company or squadron level, followed by ten days at battalion level. A further ten days had been set aside for brigade-level training if time permitted. Divisional-level exercises could only be expected if the formation was not needed at the front.

Training took place on six days out of every seven (the men were allowed Sunday off). Each battalion marched out of camp to its assigned area early in the morning, before dividing into companies. To harden up the men, each wore his full kit, including packs. One member of 5th Battalion described his experience in a letter home: 'For the first three weeks, reveille 6.15 am, breakfast 7, fall in 8. March about three miles in ankle deep sand with one bread roll per man and one tin sardines to four men for lunch (no variation in diet for lunch and breakfast, bread and jam one slice per man) return to camp at 4 pm. Training consisted of skirmishing for about two miles across the desert.' In an attempt to cram more training into daylight hours, reveille was soon moved back to 0530hrs and the return to camp delayed a further half-hour. On some days the men did not get back until midnight.

These New Zealanders take advantage of opportunities for open-air bathing at Ismailia. (Liddle Collection)

B RECRUITS IN TRAINING, AUSTRALIA, 1914

So great was the rush to enlist that it outran the supply of uniform. Contemporary photographs of men under training show that a wide mixture of service and civilian clothing was in use. Initial issues consisted of the 1912-pattern uniform, but with a khaki forage cap instead of a bush hat. There were not enough sets of the 1908 webbing to equip everyone, so many recruits were issued with a reduced set of the 1903 pattern, without the bandolier.

The sergeant has managed to retain his pre-war uniform, that of 52nd (Hobson's Bay) Battalion, based in south Melbourne. The battalion was descended from the Victorian Scottish, a militia regiment raised in 1898, and retained a large number of Scottish features in its uniform. But, despite the black braid and rank badges, this was not a rifles regiment. The tartan was specific to the regiment – it was based on the Black Watch tartan, but with an extra red overstripe. The 52nd (together with the 51st, another Melbourne battalion) saw many of its men volunteer into 5th Battalion, AIF. Photographs of former 52nd Battalion men at Gallipoli show that they continued to wear their regimental glengarry.

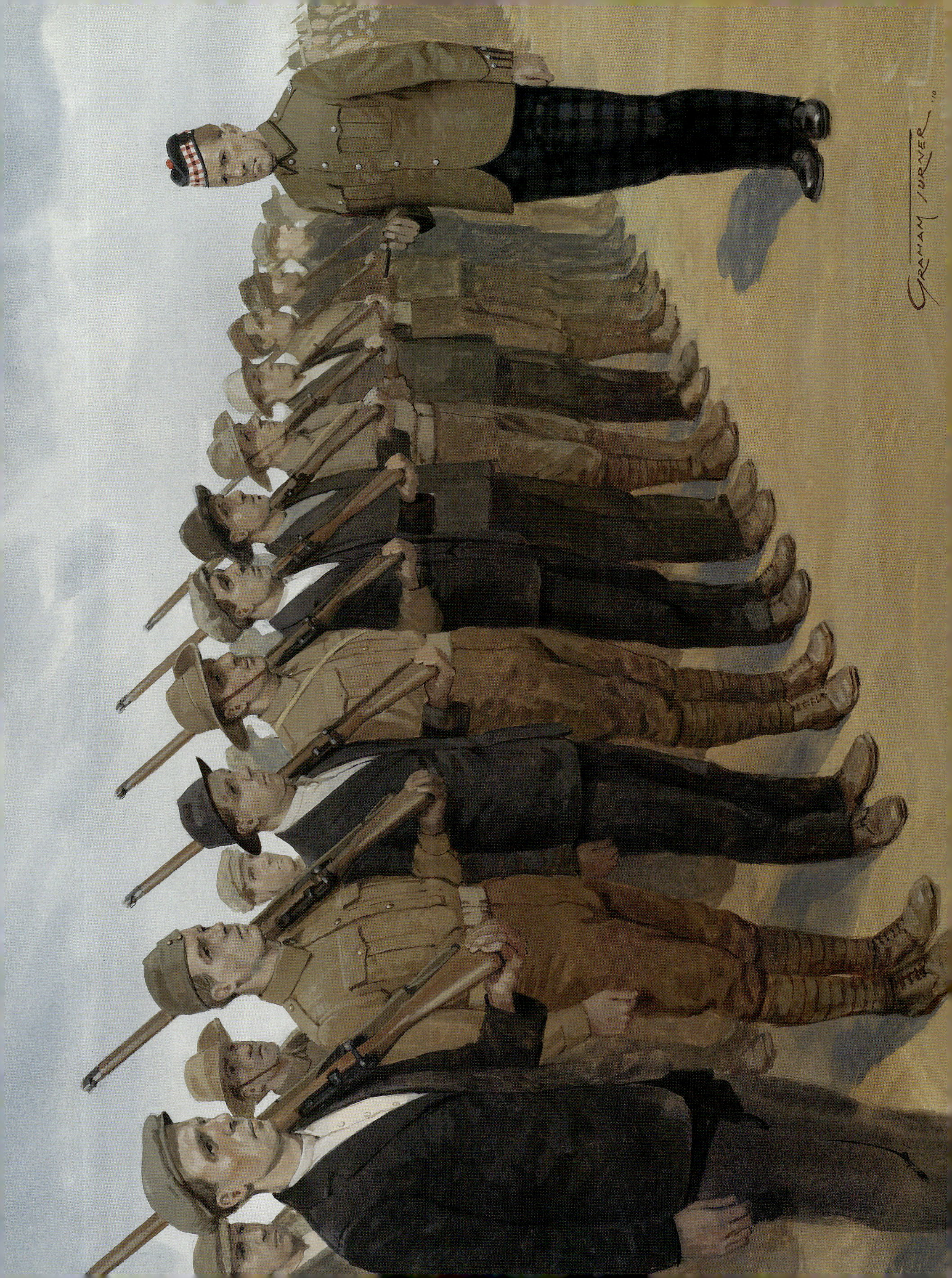
GRAHAM TURNER

Taking in the sights – Private Bill Dorrington (3rd Battalion) at the Pyramids. So entranced was one of Dorrington's comrades that he confessed he could almost forget there even was a place called Australia. (Liddle Collection)

Marching through soft sand, the Anzacs sweated a great deal. But as soon as they laid down their heavy loads they were chilled by the cold winter wind. As a result many men went down with chills and fevers. The 5th Battalion man quoted above served in a company where 43 of his comrades out of 200 paraded sick (but only 10 were excused duty).

In the event, the divisions spent longer than expected in Egypt and underwent four months of training before they were needed at the front. A complicating factor was introduced on 1 January 1915, when the British forced the Australian battalions to reorganize. Each battalion had formed on an eight-company basis, but the Australians now had to change to four 'double companies', each commanded by a major or captain, with another captain as second-in-command. Each double company was then divided into four platoons, each around 50 men strong and commanded by a subaltern. Company-level training had to be extended as a result of this, and it was not until February that battalion-level exercises took place. By the time 1st Division was sent to the Dardanelles, brigade-level field days were only just taking place.

Disappointingly, the training regime made no attempt to pass on the fruits of combat experience from the Western Front – everything was based on peacetime standards. Although it was a fit, well-drilled formation that sailed from Alexandria on 8 April 1915, the two contingents remained, in Pugsley's phrase, 'civilian armies with the barest veneer of military expertise'. Lord Kitchener was less than complimentary when he summed up the situation for Prime Minister Herbert Asquith. In his caustic opinion, the Anzacs were 'quite good enough if a cruise on the Sea of Marmara was all that was contemplated'.

For, during their time in Egypt, the Anzacs had acquired a new role. Their destination was now Turkey, specifically the Dardanelles – the narrow straits that separate Europe from Asia, and link the Mediterranean with Constantinople (Istanbul) and the Black Sea. Commanded by Major-General (Lieutenant-General from 28 October 1915) Sir William Birdwood, the Corps was to join British and French divisions in a Mediterranean Expeditionary Force, commanded by General Sir Ian Hamilton. Hamilton's plan was simple: the British and French would land on the tip of the Gallipoli peninsula, drive out the Turkish garrison and take control of the Mediterranean end of the straits. Meanwhile the Anzacs would land higher up the coast on the Turkish right flank, cross the peninsula and take the settlement of Maidos – cutting off the garrison, securing the narrow entry to the Sea of Marmara and so opening a route to Constantinople.

UNIFORM AND EQUIPMENT

Plans to uniform the AIF in the same khaki colour as the British Army (known as 'drab') soon came to nought. The only cloth on hand at the outbreak of war was a greenish 'pea soup' colour, with a softer felted surface, and this was the fabric chosen. Prolonged exposure to the elements eventually faded the jacket to a blue-grey colour – as members of the light-horse regiments serving in Sinai were also to find. Most of the early uniforms were made by private contractors, although a government factory was set up in Geelong (Victoria). The tunics also differed in detail from British patterns. The cut, for example, was more generous, particularly in the arms. These were gathered and fastened at the wrist, and there was a large box pleat down the back.

Trousers were breeches in the same fabric, tucked into puttees, or leather gaiters for mounted troops. The brown leather ankle boots were particularly esteemed and were an object of envy amongst other Imperial armies throughout the war.

The most distinctive element of the Australian uniform was the wide-brimmed slouch hat, officially the 'hat, fur felt'. Originally introduced into forces from the state of Victoria in 1885, this hat had been adopted for all units of the new Australian Army in 1903. According to regulations, it was worn with the left side pinned up, held by a hook and eye. The 'rising sun' badge of the Commonwealth of Australia was fixed to the pinned-up brim. In peacetime, the puggaree (the band running around the base of the hat) was coloured by arm of service, but this was standardized as khaki for the men of the AIF.

Plans were put in place to equip the new force with a British-style drab peaked service dress cap. The major advantage of the cap was that it required less material. But it also offered much less protection from the sun, particularly on the back of the neck, so wearers received a cloth havelock to remedy this deficiency. Some battalions, like 7th Battalion, adopted the cap from the beginning. But supplies were insufficient to equip every battalion, and many continued to favour the slouch hat. The superior sun-shading qualities of the latter, and its distinctive appearance – marking the wearer out as Antipodean at the very least – made it increasingly popular, and the cap gradually fell out of favour.

One particular item of kit bemused Sergeant Harry Kahan, of 28th Battalion. 'We started off,' he recalled, 'with flannel cholera belts with sundry tapes to fasten them round your waist… None of us would wear them. They ended up as strips of cloth to clean our rifles. I don't know how it was supposed to prevent cholera.'

A rule forbidding men from shaving their upper lip was quickly abandoned. 'Perhaps it lent an appearance of ferociousness or maturity on our childish faces,' thought Sergeant Kahan, 'but anyway that was soon forgotten and we were allowed to shave. I didn't grow a moustache because at that age I couldn't grow sufficient whiskers to cover my lip. "The Australian Eleven" it was called on us young fellows – eleven hairs growing on our upper lip.'

Making little concession to the heat, two New Zealanders wear full uniform and kit to pose for the camera under a full sun, Sidi Bishr, Egypt, 1915. (Gill Denniston Collection, Turnbull Library)

On reaching Gallipoli the troops no longer paid the same attention to regulations in matters of uniform. Here a group of weary-looking New Zealanders, believed to be Wellington Mounted Rifles, sit in their shirtsleeves, wearing a mixture of tropical helmets and forage caps. They are depicted at Table Top, preparing for the attack at Chunuk Bair on 6 August. (J. C. Read Collection, Turnbull Library)

The infantry wore the 1908 webbing equipment, and mounted troops wore the leather 1903 bandolier equipment. This was practical and useful, but recruits took some time to get used to its intricacies. 'The average platoon could have the entire Sahara Desert to lay the web out on,' noted the historian of 5th Battalion, 'and still emerge a sweating, swearing mass to find that besides having assembled it altogether wrongly, each one had either taken some of the next man's part or in some devilish inexplicable way had buckled their kit on to his. The inventor probably died insane.'

Most of the initial issue of personal equipment came from British stores – heliographs, enamelled water bottles, bits, stirrups, spurs and shovels – until Australian production managed to catch up. The saddlery and harnesses of

C · THE AUSTRALIAN SOLDIER

A man kitted out exactly as the quartermaster would wish to see him. The jacket was a pattern designed especially for the AIF, using experience gained from the 'military shirt' of the Citizen Military Forces (depicted in the artwork on p. 15). The new jacket was based on British patterns, but the sleeves were made much roomier, and were buttoned at the cuff. The trousers were identical in style to the pre-war dismounted-pattern breeches. Standard equipment was the 1908 webbing set. The men carried the SMLE rifle.

No allowance was made for battalion badges. All members of the AIF wore a shoulder title bearing the single word 'Australia', while their headgear carried either the sunburst badge (**1**) or the badge of the Royal Australian Artillery. However, while the AIF was in Egypt in 1915, a system of cloth badges was introduced. The shape identified the division, and the colour identified the battalion within the division and its state of origin. The badges were usually worn on the upper sleeve. However, John Monash, the commanding officer of 4th Infantry Brigade, instructed his men to wear their badges on their hats. The patches illustrated are those of 25th Battalion (a diamond for 2nd Division and blue for Queensland) (**2**), 2nd Battalion (a rectangle for 1st Division and green for New South Wales) (**3**) and 1st Light Horse (**4**).

Many weapons had to be improvised on the beachhead itself. Grenades were a prime example, among them the 'jam-tin grenade' (officially, the Double Cylinder No. 8 or No. 9, depending on its size and composition) (**5**) and the 'butterpat grenade' (officially, the No. 12) (**6**). These were later supplemented by the 'cricket-ball' or 'Malta' grenade (**7**). This was manufactured in quantity and adopted as the No. 15 grenade. It was rather too large to use easily, and the case fragmented into pieces that were deemed too small. Some use was also made of rifle grenades, including the 1915 No. 3 Mk. I (**8**). This was, however, time-consuming to manufacture, and difficult to use with any degree of accuracy.

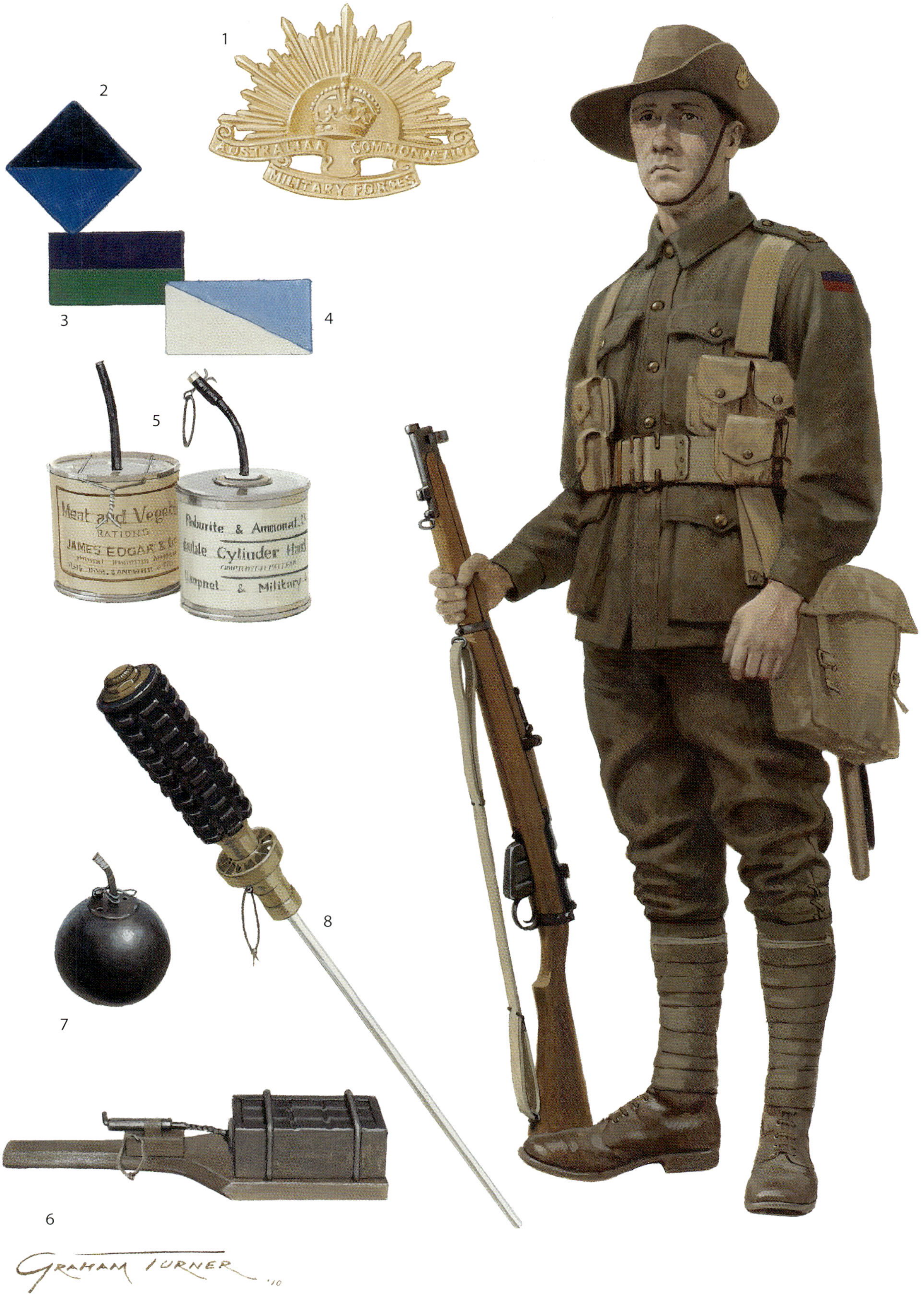
1
MILITARY FORCES
2
3
4
5
RATIONS
6
7
8
GRAHAM TURNER

BELOW
Gas masks were issued to the men, but fears of Turkish gas attacks proved unfounded. (Gill Denniston Collection, Turnbull Library)

BELOW RIGHT
A sniper in action, aiming his periscope rifle, while his partner observes through a periscope. 'I have been sniping,' wrote one Australian, 'and had some very good sport … it is an exciting game, far more than football.' (Suzanne Duncan Collection, Turnbull Library)

the light-horse regiments were produced by the Government Harness Factory at Clifton Hill (Victoria).

The AIF was armed with the British Short Magazine Lee-Enfield (SMLE) Mk. III, firing the older Mk. VI ammunition (the British were moving to the newer, high-velocity Mk. VII rounds). A factory had been constructed at Lithgow (New South Wales) in 1912 to make these weapons, but it was only producing 15,000 guns a year in 1913 – insufficient for the AIF battalions forming at the outbreak of war. The initial issue, to the tune of 87,240 weapons, was made possible only by taking guns from Citizen Forces stocks. At the end of 1914, the Lithgow factory expanded its production to 35,000 weapons a year, and it would go on to make 25 per cent of all the rifles taken overseas. Ammunition came from the Commonwealth Cordite Factory at Maribyrnong (Victoria), the Colonial Ammunition Company (Auckland), and from Britain.

New Zealand's troops were dressed as their British counterparts. The infantrymen retained their 'long' Lee-Enfields, bought from Canada and Britain, throughout the Gallipoli campaign; they started to receive quantities of Lithgow-made SMLEs only while refitting in Egypt in 1916. However, the artillery and Mounted Rifles troops were issued with SMLEs from the start. Whatever weapon he carried, the Anzac position on the Gallipoli peninsula was so precarious that every man kept his bayonet fixed at all times.

The sniping war on the peninsula led to a number of innovations – some improvised, others of regulation issue. A small number of scoped rifles were supplied later in the campaign to help combat Turkish snipers, although some Anzac snipers, such as Queenslander Private Billy Sing, preferred to rely on the rifle's own 'iron' sights. One of the improvised inventions was the 'Wallaby sniping cage' – a frame to hold the rifle. Once the sniper had hit an enemy loophole, he could lock his rifle into position and fire again without needing to take aim.

A New Zealand machine gunner engages the enemy, while another observes through a periscope. (Queen Elizabeth II Army Memorial Museum Collection, Turnbull Library)

Periscopes were also in common use. The 2nd Field Company, Australian Engineers, started to make them from pieces of mirror on a stick, and by the end of May 1915 they had produced 3,000. But the Turks soon learned to look out for the periscopes, and by July 1st Division was losing about 30 a day. A refinement was the periscope rifle, invented by Lance Corporal W. C. Beech of 2nd Battalion. These specially adapted weapons restored firepower to posts where the firer found it impossible to show himself at a loophole.

Each battalion also included two .303in. Maxim guns, used largely at the initiative of battalion commanding officers. By the end of 1915 the British Army was forming brigade machine-gun companies to concentrate the fire of these weapons; but developments at Gallipoli had already anticipated this. As early as May 1915, Captain J. C. Rose, a New Zealander commanding the guns of 4th Australian Brigade, was already organizing them to provide mutually supporting arcs of fire, and so dominate the front of their position. The light horse were armed with older .45in. Maxim guns and retained them throughout the Gallipoli campaign; they would not receive Hotchkiss machine guns until 1917.

A New Zealand soldier inserts fuses into jam-tin bombs. (Gill Denniston Collection, Turnbull Library)

Unlike the Turks, the Anzacs had no experience of hand grenades. Needing some swift improvisation, jam tins were quickly set aside and filled with fragments of shells, pieces of barbed wire, stones and nails; a fuse and detonator attached to a piece of gun-cotton completed the weapon. The first jam-tin grenade was issued on 4 June. They worked best when thrown from trench to trench. At a forward position like Quinn's Post, bombing could go on all through the night.

Some units were issued with 'cricket-ball bombs' (or 'Malta bombs', from their place of manufacture), ignited by striking the fuse on a match-striker sewn onto the left side of the tunic. Yet others received Lotbinière bombs, named after their inventor, Birdwood's chief engineer, which consisted of a slab of explosive attached to a wooden paddle. Sergeant Major Norman Worrall (8th Light Horse) was serving at Russell's Top when he first saw the new weapon. 'We tried a new style of bomb called the "Butterpat",' he recorded in his diary.

'It consists of two and a half lbs of gun cotton and a two-seconds fuse wired onto a piece of board with a handle like a butter pat. These were discharged from No. 2 Sap, which is only 15 yards from the enemy's trench. The result was more than we expected. Earth was thrown from the Turk's trench back into our firing line, 40 yards away, the earth shook as from an earthquake tremor.' But only ten men in each company received training as bombers, and then only once they reached the peninsula. No training of this type was undertaken in Egypt, not even for reinforcements.

The power of the human arm was supplemented when needed by a range of locally produced catapults. But the accuracy of these improvised weapons left a lot to be desired. 'Somewhere down the Rhododendron Spur', recalled Private Alexander Aitken of the Otagos, 'the Australians had improvised a bomb-throwing catapult, but very erratic and feared by us, I fancy, more than by the Turks.'

The Australians could also call on a small number of trench mortars, a weapon in its infancy at this period of the war. Four Japanese-made mortars were supplied to the Anzacs, two per division. The men of 5th Light Horse began to train with one in Egypt in early May. 'Sounds rather a big thing but two men can carry it and it takes three to work it. Has a range of 400 yards throwing a 4lb bomb of high explosives,' commented one member of the regiment. The first trench mortar arrived on the peninsula around 22 May and was dispatched to Courtney's Post. But ammunition was in short supply. Only 2,000 rounds came with the weapon – any more would have to be

D NEW ZEALAND SOLDIER

The hat worn by the New Zealanders was similar to the Australian pattern, but crushed into a different shape. This idiosyncrasy had originated in 1911, when the 11th Taranaki Rifles pushed the crown of the hat upwards to stop rain collecting in the creases during a particularly wet annual camp, and the change was made official in the regiment shortly thereafter. When a cadre of former Taranaki officers and NCOs joined the Wellington Battalion of the New Zealand Expeditionary Force, the style was introduced into that battalion; from there, it spread to the rest of the force and ultimately the rest of the New Zealand Army. Some battalions wore the hat in the Australian style, with the brim fastened up on the left; meanwhile, troopers of the Mounted Rifles tended to wear the brim down, with a front-to-back indentation in the crown (a style made official in 1916). It seems likely that these differences were encouraged to allow New Zealand soldiers to be distinguished from Australians. The puggarees were coloured according to arm of service – for example, khaki with a red central fold for the infantry, or khaki with a green central fold for the Mounted Rifles. Some men were issued with a Wolseley sun helmet, while others received a forage cap.

The tunic was the New Zealand-manufactured 1902 khaki pattern, which was similar to British service dress. In Egypt, this was sometimes replaced by a lighter, khaki drill tunic.

With insufficient SMLEs available, the New Zealand infantry went to war armed with 'Long' Lee-Enfields instead. The short version was not issued until after the Gallipoli campaign. The infantry wore British-pattern webbing, but the Mounted Rifles were equipped with the uncomfortable New Zealand 1905 bandolier equipment. In the beachhead, the latter was replaced by webbing wherever possible.

Both Australians and New Zealanders used the obsolete Maxim machine gun. In the fighting on Chunuk Bair, an Otago man of 5th Reinforcements exhibited extraordinary sangfroid during a Turkish attack. He 'was working in front of where the gun took up position. He was told to stop work when the gun was ready and to crouch down so that the gun could fire over him. Against all the rules of war he immediately lighted [sic] his pipe. The Turks, only 80 yards (73m) away, opened fire with about 20 rifles on to the light. Their rifle flashes disclosed their position and the machine-gun drove them out.'

The Garland trench mortar was another weapon improvised on the beachhead. It consisted of a tempered steel barrel (65mm calibre) bolted onto a solid wooden base-plate at an angle of 45 degrees. It had to be aimed by turning the whole mortar, and the only means of lengthening the range was to prop the base-plate up on something, such as a box.

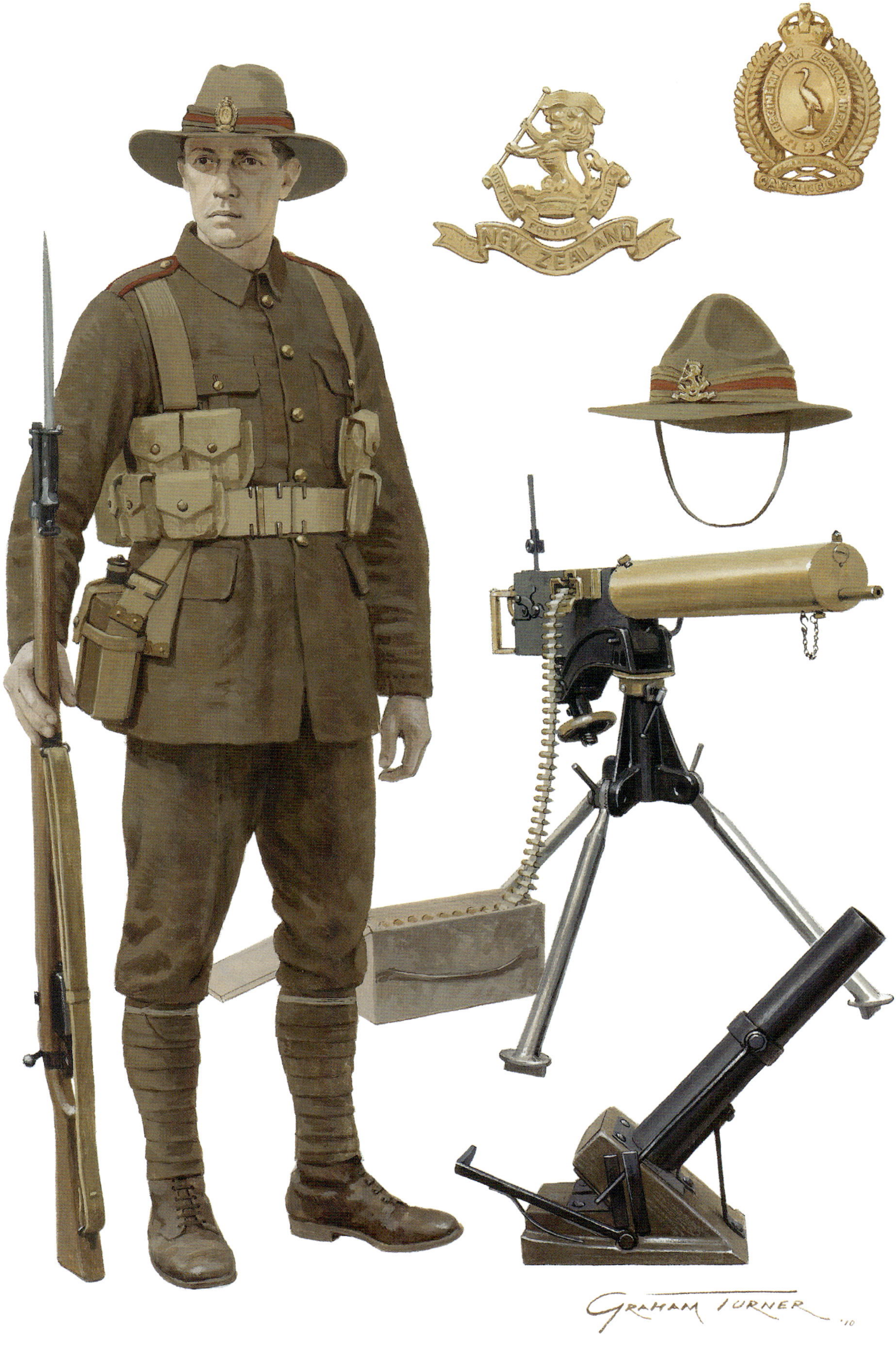
NEW ZEALAND
GRAHAM TURNER '10

A grenade-throwing catapult, improvised by the New Zealanders. Some thought that these contraptions posed a greater danger to their own side than they did to the Turks. (Thomas Stout Collection, Turnbull Library)

specially manufactured in Japan – and by October 1st Division had exhausted its stocks.

The Anzacs once again improvised a weapon to fill the gap. The Garland mortar was a plain steel barrel of 65mm calibre, fixed at an angle of 45 degrees on a plain wooden base. The bombs it fired were little more than variants of the jam-tin grenade, but with a white calico tail attached to improve their accuracy. These Garland mortars were slightly more plentiful than the conventional trench mortars – 1st Division had acquired seven tubes by October – and there was no lack of bombs to fire.

Ammunition was not the only thing in short supply. Shortages of basic material such as medical, trench and engineering stores dogged the campaign. The Anzacs had to improvise far too much on the beachhead (or indeed steal if zealous quartermasters refused to release much-needed stores without the proper authorization). Some battalions were reduced to buying field telephones from Britain out of regimental funds because none were available on the peninsula.

The nature of the terrain around the beachhead made it very difficult for the infantry to obtain artillery support. Some guns were dragged into the front line on Plugge's Plateau to fire over open sights. Here a New Zealand crew poses for the camera. (Liddle Collection)

Artillery support came from a New Zealand 4.5in. howitzer battery (which fired live ammunition for the first time with its opening round on 26 April), an Indian mountain battery and Australian and New Zealand 18-pdr batteries. But the shortages endemic to the Gallipoli campaign hit the artillery too. The howitzers were limited to only two rounds a day, and the 18-pdrs to somewhere between 10 and 20 shrapnel rounds (for there were no high-explosive rounds available). Meanwhile, the steep cliffs around Anzac Cove posed more problems for the guns, making it hard for them to achieve the elevation needed to provide fire support to the forward lines. A number were dragged to the top of Plugge's Plateau and fired over open sights, but points like this were few. The powerful guns of the naval vessels anchored offshore were also stymied by the terrain. The low trajectory of their fire limited its effectiveness, and they could only engage targets on the forward slopes of the Turkish positions.

STRAIGHT INTO ACTION

As they drew closer to the enemy shore early in the morning of 25 April, some of the men in the boats were struck by the stillness of the scene. Lieutenant Ivor Margetts, a Tasmanian serving with 12th Battalion, recalled: 'I am quite sure few of us realized that at last we were actually bound for our baptism of fire for it seemed as though we were just out on one of our night manoeuvres in Mudros harbour, but very soon we realized it was neither a surprise party nor a moonlight picnic.' For others the predominant memory of the 40-minute trip from the transports to the landing beach was how long it seemed: 'like days' for Sergeant Henry Cheney (10th Battalion) and 'to go on for ever' for Lieutenant Aubrey Darnell (11th Battalion).

However tough their training regime, it had done nothing to prepare the Anzacs for the shock of landing under fire that morning. The leading boats were within 20m of the shore when the Turks opened fire. Reginald Nicholas, a Perth man serving with the Hospital Transport Corps, described the scene: 'Our boys had to jump over the side of boats into the water, in some places

Men of the Australian contingent – probably from A and C Companies, 3rd Battalion – sail towards the landings on board the British battleship HMS *London*. (Liddle Collection)

up to the armpits ... men [were] killed in the boats and in the water ... looking down at the bottom of the sea, you could see a carpet of dead men ... shot getting out of the boats.'

Another Western Australian shared similar memories. Private (later CSM) George Feist of 12th Battalion recalled:

> I was in the second tow, and we got it, shrapnel and rifle fire bad. We lost three on the destroyer and four in the boat getting to land. The Turks were close on the beach when we got there. We had to fix bayonets and charge. We jumped into the water up to our waists and some ... their armpits ... we had to trust to the penknife at the end of our rifles. When I got there it was not too long, but ... I tell you you do not forget these things ... all we thought of was to get at them. One would hear someone say 'They've got me' and register another notch when you get to them, that's all.

The Anzacs landed in 12 'tows'. Consisting of a picket boat, a steam launch or pinnace, a cutter and a lifeboat, each tow was capable of carrying 120–60 men. The steam launch brought them as close as possible to the shore, and then cutters rowed them to the beach. Hamilton had requested more boats, but in vain. He could land only two divisions at a time, the boats then returning to the transports to collect the follow-up waves. The brigades and battalions of the assault force had rehearsed the landing on the nearby Aegean island of Lemnos from 15 to 18 April. There they were told: 'no rifle fire is to be employed until broad daylight. The bayonet only is to be used. No bugle calls are to be sounded after leaving Lemnos. No bugle calls are to be sounded during the charge.' But, under the circumstances, this was a counsel of perfection. Of all the battalions in the assault force, the men of 11th Battalion appear to have met the heaviest fire as they approached the beach, and they were 'shouting and hurraying and calling the Turks all the rude names they could think of'.

'Straight up that rugged, rocky precipice we went,' recalled Henry Cheney. And this despite the burden they were carrying: a full pack, three sandbags, three days' worth of tinned rations and up to 200 rounds of ammunition –

The landings are seen here as viewed from HMS *Prince of Wales* by a member of the ship's company. (Liddle Collection)

for most men somewhere around 75lb (34kg) in weight. Tom Usher, a Queenslander, served with 9th Battalion:

> You're up to your neck in water – and a lot of them got drowned, too, with the weight of their packs and that – then scramble ashore and take shelter as quick as you could. You're only looking after yourself, you couldn't worry about the other bloke, you had to get ashore as quick as you could – just keep your rifle above your head, keep it dry… I could see these cliffs, and I ran for it. You didn't care who you were with as long as you got away from the fire.

In planning the operation, Anzac commanders had identified two potential landing places – one on either side of the Gaba Tepe headland. To the south of this headland lay a wide bay with a shallow sloping beach, but it was heavily defended from a nearby ridge. The alternative was a much more confined bay to the north. The beach there was narrow and dominated by steep slopes immediately to its rear. It was, however, less well defended, and this was where the landing took place.

The choice remains controversial to this day. It appears that the original plan envisaged a landing on the southern beach, with one proviso. If the landing boats came under fire during their approach then the more northerly beach could be used. But the confusion of a night-time approach, last-minute changes of course, the difficulty of identifying the correct headland, poor Admiralty maps, and apprehension about Turkish fire all contributed to an unplanned drift northwards by the landing boats.

Once the Anzacs had alighted on the northern beach, the die was cast. The difficult rugged landscape soon brought the landing into confusion, and coordinated movement proved impossible. Soldiers were unable to see ahead without standing up, but doing so simply invited a sniper's bullet, or a piece of shrapnel. Casualties were particularly heavy amongst officers and NCOs, leaving their men to fend for themselves. 'Many of our officers were shot down,' recalled Ray Baker (9th Battalion), 'and most of the time we got no orders at all but had to rely on ourselves to do the best we could.'

Their 'best' was very limited. All they could do was make short dashes forward under heavy artillery and small-arms fire. George Mitchell (10th Battalion) described: 'a scramble, a rapid pounding of heavy boots and clattering of equipment, a startled yell and a crumpling body which has to be

The New Zealanders of Auckland Battalion came ashore later in the morning of 25 April. 'I turned round and took [this picture] as soon as I landed,' noted the photographer, Sergeant George May. (Liddle Collection)

The heavy line marks the farthest extent of the trenches occupied by the Anzacs. The Corps' northern boundary ran just to the north of the Azmak Dere watercourse. (Author's collection)

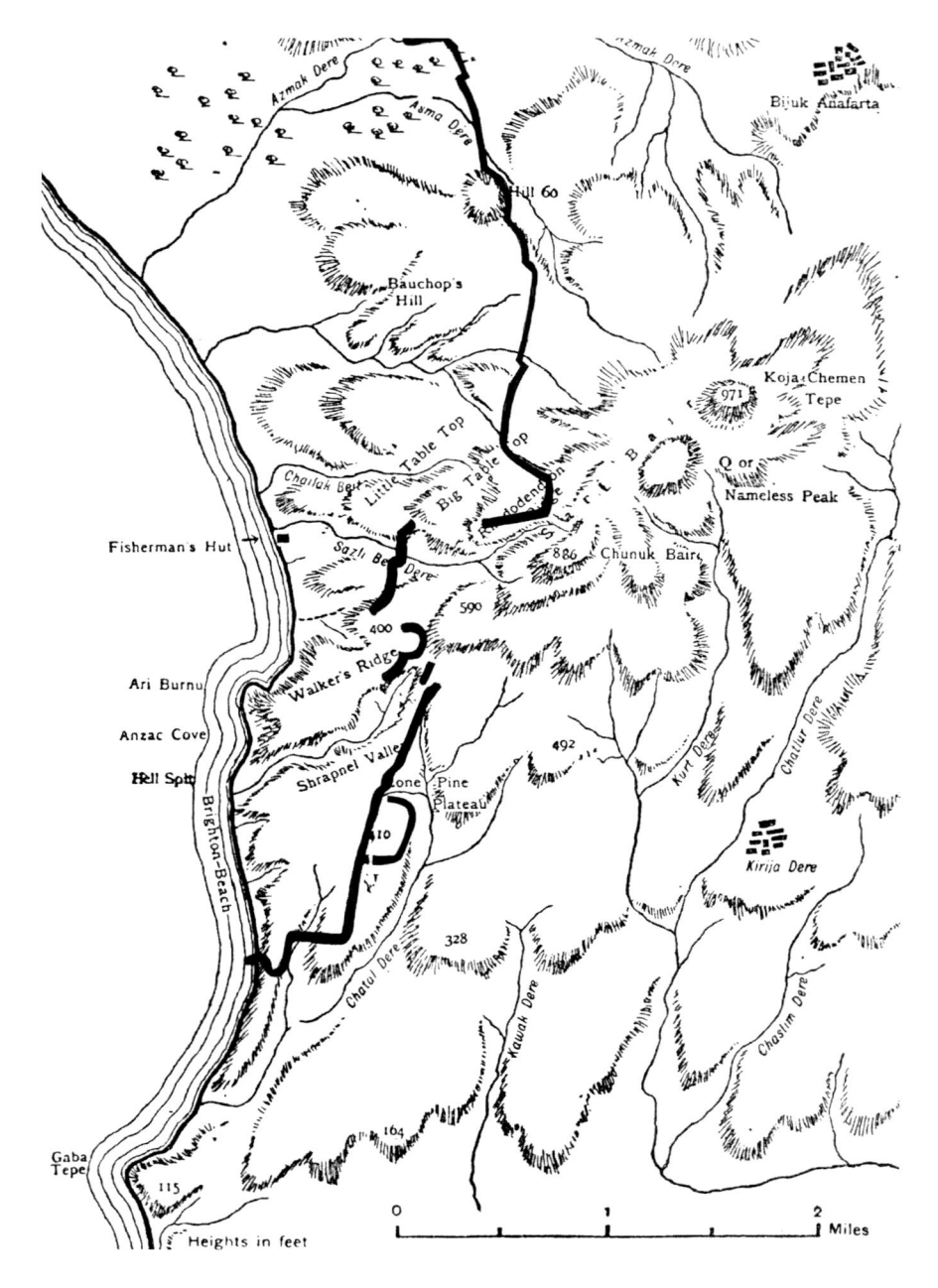

leaped over, a succession of slithering thuds, and [then] we are down in the bushes forty yards ahead.' Writing home, his 10th Battalion comrade William Welch summed things up with consummate understatement: 'My word, what a mix-up it was.'

Without command or control, men made their own decision to advance, and their enthusiasm took them beyond the reach of their supports. Birdwood later bemoaned their eagerness. His men had gone forward with 'too much dash,' he said, 'for they took on more than they could manage, dashing away to the extreme spurs of the hills which were much too extended to hold … but then the most awful reaction followed.' A number of men returned to the beachhead on their own initiative, serving only to deepen the confusion.

Where was the front line? What was its condition? The Anzac hold on the landing areas was so tenuous that for a time senior commanders contemplated evacuation. But in the end they decided to hang on.

Jack Jensen served with 1st Battalion. His platoon landed later in the day but suffered along with the others: 'As soon as we got on the beach a shell fell right into my platoon and killed one and wounded six, three of whom died afterwards from the wounds… A few yards further another shell dropped among us knocking over nine or ten the officer included. About two hours afterwards when they made a count there was only thirteen left out of fifty.' The commanding officer of the Aucklands, also part of the follow-up waves, was a little luckier. He was surprised to find 'how peaceful was our trip ashore … a little shelling. Some dropping rifle fire but only two casualties in our battalion. The landing was peaceful but distinctly wet, particularly for us small ones. It is surprising what a lot of water a ship's boat draws. The quietness of our narrow strip of beach was also surprising. A few Australians forming up; an Indian mountain battery and some wounded and dying men.'

Looking back, the Anzacs were astonished by what they achieved that day. One later reinforcement sums up the general view: 'The more I see of this inhospitable place, the more I marvel that any survived. The original men must have been a combination of mule, goat and lion, to have succeeded as they did.' Approximately 4,000 men had landed by 0500hrs, 8,000 by 0800hrs and 15,000 by 1800hrs. Casualties numbered roughly 2,000, of whom around 500 were killed.

Once the initial landing had achieved a toehold on the peninsula, the campaign descended into stalemate. The Anzacs were not strong enough to advance farther, but the Turks were unable to drive the enemy back into the sea. In some places, only a matter of yards separated the two opposing lines of trenches. Strongpoints like Quinn's Post, Courtney's Post and Johnston's Jolly saw continual low-intensity action as snipers from both sides stalked their prey, and grenades flew back and forth. Cecil Malthus (Canterbury Battalion) described his time at Quinn's Post: 'To lie cowering in the darkness of the cramped and evil-smelling pit and watch a big bomb sputtering among the corpses just against our loophole while waiting for the burst was an experience that no man could endure unmoved.'

The more agile were able to throw the bombs back while their primitive fuses were still burning, but this was no simple matter. 'The trouble was', noted one officer of the Wellington Mounted Rifles, 'that the explosions deafened us so much that after a time we could not hear where the bombs were falling and then the strain was pretty bad. The trenches were pretty narrow and a man had to be careful not to get stuck when either reaching for a bomb or getting away. Wounded men lying in the bottom of the trenches were really the worst sufferers from bombs.'

Digging provided the best protection (the nickname 'Digger' would come later – at the time, Australians were 'Aussies' or 'Cornstalks', while the New Zealanders were the 'Enzedders' or the

Soldiers of 2nd Division in the trench at Lone Pine. One man uses a mirror attached to a long stick to observe the Turkish trenches, while his comrades gather round. The man at the rear has written 'Colac', the name of his home town in Victoria, on his hat. (Liddle Collection)

In early May, the New Zealand Infantry Brigade and 2nd Australian Brigade were temporarily transferred to the Cape Helles front to support an offensive there (the Second Battle of Krithia). The location seen here was known as the Daisy Patch. 'I was under that tree for some time and bullets were cutting off branches in fine style,' recalled George May. (Liddle Collection)

'Fernleaves'). Personal scrapes were joined together to form larger dugouts, which in turn were widened and deepened into trenches. Where the ground permitted, the Anzacs then turned these trenches into tunnels, providing some sort of overhead shelter for their occupants. According to Bean some of them resembled, 'a sort of ditch cut, somewhere between a grave and a cave, into the creek side'. Like his mates, one New Zealander soon turned digger: 'Wright and I in our spare time worked hard at a new bivvy – everybody was doing the same. We first made terraces and then went in as far as possible, getting at least 15 feet [4.57m] of rock overhead to be safe against the heavy shells which were expected before long. We called these "funk holes", a name however very unpopular with our Colonel, who decried its use.'

Trench life was not for the claustrophobic. Lance Corporal Leonard Mitchell of the Otagos emphasized just how cramped they were: 'Most of the men are accommodated in dug-outs and recesses, undercut at the bottom of gaps or communications trenches 8 or 9 feet [2.44–2.74m] below the surface,' he wrote. 'Each dug-out is 10 feet long with two side recesses on each side… This holds eight men, two in each side recess. Each recess is 3' 6"[1.07m] high, 3' 6" [1.07m] wide, 6' [1.83m] long, so the men have to lie down always.'

Only in November did the Turks finally gain the upper hand, by bringing up a battery of four Austrian howitzers. These powerful weapons bombarded Lone Pine, causing heavy casualties and considerable damage, and doubtless influenced the decision to evacuate the beachhead a month later.

E IN THE TRENCHES

Dress regulations were not strictly enforced, either by the Australians or by the New Zealanders, and contemporary photographs show groups of men all dressed slightly differently. Not all of these changes were deliberate – in the field, wear and tear on clothing could be excessive and resupply often slow, so men simply made the best of it. The Australian C. E. W. Bean, always dismissive of the New Zealanders, claimed that they just wanted to be Australians: 'The N.Z. men half consciously came to imitate the Australians, e.g. the Australian language was about five times as strong as that of the N.Z.s – but the N.Z.s came to adopt it. The Sydney men followed the Sydney custom of trying to get their backs and skins as brown as possible through sun-baking. The N.Z.s followed them – they were often blacker than Turks and blacker than Indians before the summer was over.' One Egyptian newspaper commented rather primly: 'Not since the prehistoric stone ages has such a naked army been seen in civilised warfare as the Australian army corps fighting on the Gallipoli Peninsula. They display an utter abhorrence for superfluous clothing. They are famous throughout Europe for their hard fighting, hard swearing and nakedness, even to a sense of indecency.'

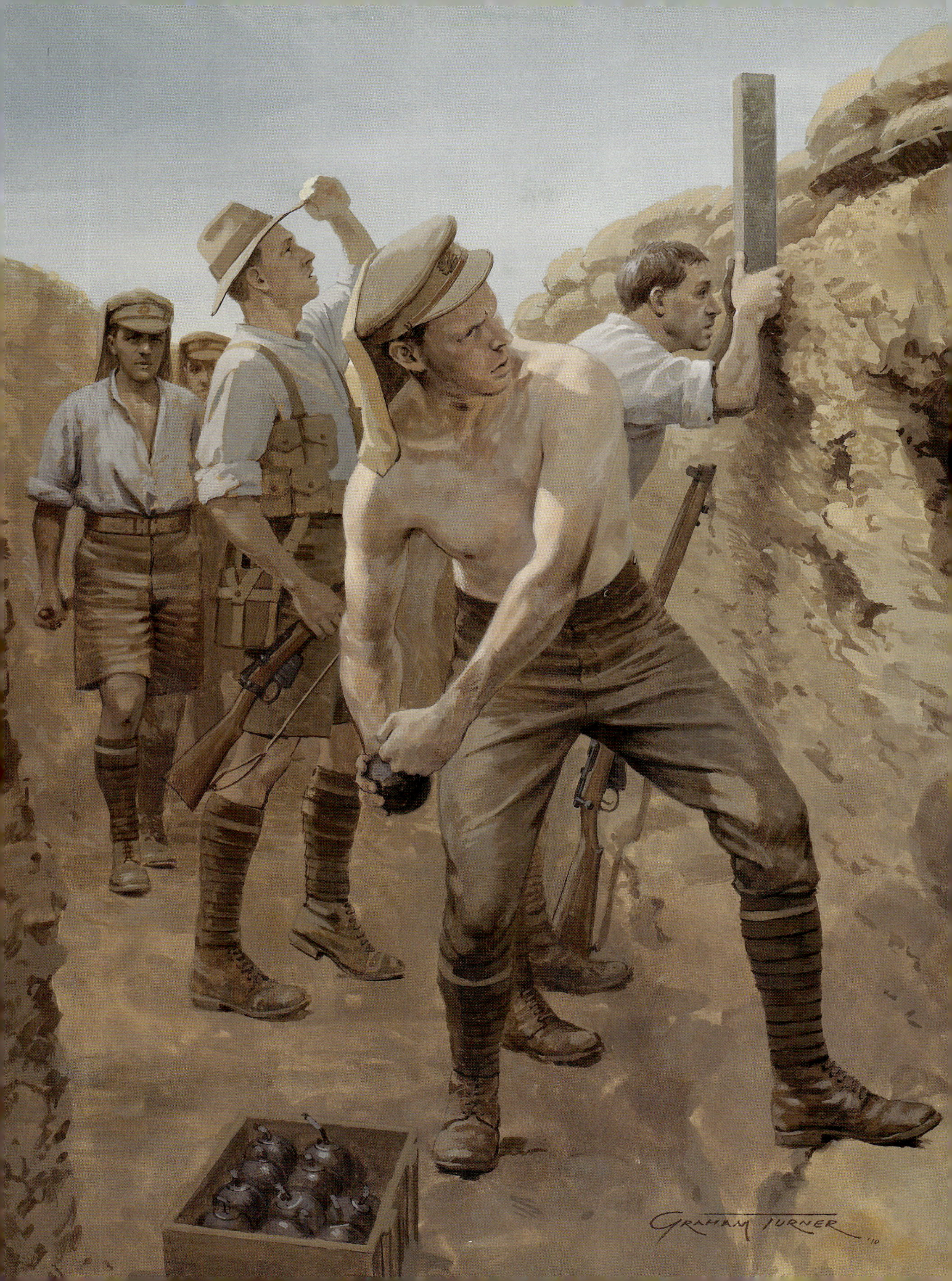
GRAHAM TURNER

ABOVE
A New Zealand dugout. On such a confined site, dugouts were always crowded. (James Hutchison Collection, Turnbull Library)

ABOVE RIGHT
'Stirring up a sniper,' read the original caption to this photo. The men of 5th Light Horse attempt to bring some suppressing fire onto the position occupied by the sniper. (Liddle Collection)

Turkish snipers troubled the Anzacs from the moment they set foot on the peninsula. Any attempt to move water, rations and ammunition from the beachhead to the front line was a perilous business, particularly in the main arteries like Monash Gully. The introduction of the periscope rifle provided some protection for the soldiers in the trenches, enabling them to retaliate without the need to expose themselves to danger. A team of marksmen – from both Australia and New Zealand – was assembled under the command of Lieutenant T. P. 'Maori' Grace of the Wellington Battalion to take on the enemy snipers. By late June they had cleared the Turkish snipers from many of their hideouts, making resupply a much less dangerous operation.

Some battalion commanders, among them Lieutenant-Colonel Malone of the Wellingtons, were keen to dominate no man's land. First at Courtney's Post, then at Quinn's Post, he organized his defences and strengthened their layout – providing wire netting over the trenches to deflect enemy hand-grenades, deepening the shelters and improving the sanitary arrangements. He ordered his men to return three grenades for every enemy missile received, and counter

Some Anzacs did not even enjoy the luxury of a proper dugout. Here, at Pope's Post, on the evening of 6 August – just before the battle of Sari Bair – men have placed canopies over scrapes in the hillsides to improvise shelters. (E. N. Merrington Collection, Turnbull Library)

every Turkish round with rapid fire from rifles and machine guns. The then novel system of positioning machine-guns with overlapping fields of fire covered the no man's land in front of the head of Monash Gully and helped to ensure the defeat of the Turkish counter-attacks in May.

In August, the Anzacs mounted a number of coordinated attacks at Lone Pine, Quinn's Post and the Nek, and on Chunuk Bair. This series of feints and major efforts was designed to capture significant areas of high ground and potentially clear the way for the breakout from the beachhead. Lieutenant William Cameron of 9th Light Horse realized something was in the air a couple of days before the attack on the Nek. 'Ere another entry is made in this book we will have passed through a very trying time,' reads his diary entry for 5 August.

Charles Duke took part in the August attacks with his mates in 4th Battalion. 'The tension as we waited for the whistle was unbearable,' he recalled. 'We had some 70 or 80 yards to go and as the fire grew hotter we might have been doubling over crisp straw as this was the impression the noise of the firing made on me.' That day 4th Battalion lost 474 men out of a complement of 742.

Thomas McKinley of 8th Battalion had set off from Melbourne only in June. 'The noise was unbearable,' he wrote, 'and as it was my first experience in a battle you can imagine my feelings and thoughts, with no time to look around but look straight and fire straight.' 'We knew we hadn't a ghost of a chance but we charged,' remembered Trooper John Garratt of 1st Light Horse. 'We crept on,' said New South Welshman Wesley Percival of 10th Light Horse, 'scrambling and slipping on rugged slopes and across huge crevices in whose depths were often reposed the unheeded bodies of the dead, enemy and friend mixed, the result of that bloody struggle up steep hill-sides exposed to the spray of machine bullets and shrapnel.'

Seven Victoria Crosses (VCs) were won at Lone Pine alone, but there could have been many more. Describing the assault on Hill 971, Percival observed: 'of the whole of those good comrades who were with me I can honestly say that these lads performed deeds of heroism and utter fearless bravery sufficient to warrant the issue all round of VCs, but nobody of high enough military rank saw them.' Corporal Cyril Bassett was of similar mind. Bassett was a signaller with the New Zealand Engineers, and received a VC for gallantry in the assault on Chunuk Bair. 'When I got the medal I was disappointed to

Inside their artillery dugout these New Zealanders appear very tense. The man in the centre wears the earphones of a wireless set. (Liddle Collection)

find I was the only New Zealander to get one at Gallipoli,' he said, 'because hundreds of Victoria Crosses should have been awarded there.' He never mentioned his own award to his children because 'all his mates ever got were wooden crosses'.

The attack at the Nek by 8th and 10th Light Horse, immortalized in the film *Gallipoli*, was just as bloody as the assault on Lone Pine. Not one member of the two regiments reached the Turkish trenches alive. One trooper wondered how the handful of survivors had lived through the day:

> They knew they had to charge in the morn, so [they] all had their packs ready to bring back if wounded and each man prepared himself. They had a chain and a half [30m] to go to reach the Turk trenches, and got the order at 4.30 just as day was breaking. A number got killed before they got clear of our trenches ... others rushed on some running about half way, lying down then rushing on again. In the first charge only two reached the Turks... Two more lots of men ... tried to get across but got mowed down... They knew the risk before going out as it was the maddest idea to attempt it and there was not a single shirker.

Vic Nicholson of the Wellington Battalion recalled the desperate nature of the fighting when the Turks counter-attacked on Chunuk Bair:

> The bayonet fighting seemed to last weeks; I suppose it was only minutes. No one likes bayonets, and the Turks seemed to like them less than us. I don't remember any charges. It was all stand and defend with the bayonet, just a mad whirl. In the back of my head I could hear the words, 'Get the bastard before he gets you. Get him or he'll get you!' That was the fact of the matter. I don't remember bayonets going in. Perhaps I shut my eyes. I don't know who I killed and who I didn't.

What part did fear have to play amid such mayhem? 'Scared?' said Vic Nicholson. 'Sometimes you were too scared to be scared.' His compatriot Harry Browne also took part in the assault on Chunuk Bair, with the

---

F

A TRENCH ASSAULT

The experience of campaigning soon led the Anzacs into making a number of unofficial changes in the way they wore their uniform. These members of a light-horse regiment serving as infantry, and depicted charging towards the enemy trenches, show some of them. The light horse had always worn the brims of their bush hats down, adding an emu-feather plume, normally worn on the left side (mischievously, they told gullible British soldiers that the plumes were 'kangaroo feathers'). Many light horsemen retained the white puggaree of the cavalry, rather than replace it with the standard khaki. Their tunic was similar to that worn by the infantry; but their breeches were closer cut for riding, and they wore leather Strohwasser leggings instead of puttees. Their equipment was the 1903 bandolier equipment, as modified in 1905.

Many of these men have abandoned strict adherence to dress regulations in the hot Turkish summer, wearing shirtsleeves rather than a tunic, and cutting down their breeches to shorts. Trooper Fred Garrett of 3rd Light Horse commented: 'Knickerbockers are very fashionable too and most of us have cut down our infantry trews at the knees. As my knicks are fairly baggy I can quite realise what it feels like to wear kilts. Especially if one has to stand to Arms as we do at 3.30 a.m. every morning.' The men also wear the waistbelt and bandolier from the 1903 equipment set.

Yet a few days after cutting his breeches down to 'knickerbockers', Garrett was happily noting: 'I got a pair of worsted socks and flannel shirt. All Tommie clobber. Could have got a pair of slacks and a drill jacket, had I cared. Also boots, big heavy black ones with horseshoes on heals [sic], and big studs all over them. Fine footwear. As far as our material comforts are concerned it is an [sic] impossible to growl, plenty of everything.'

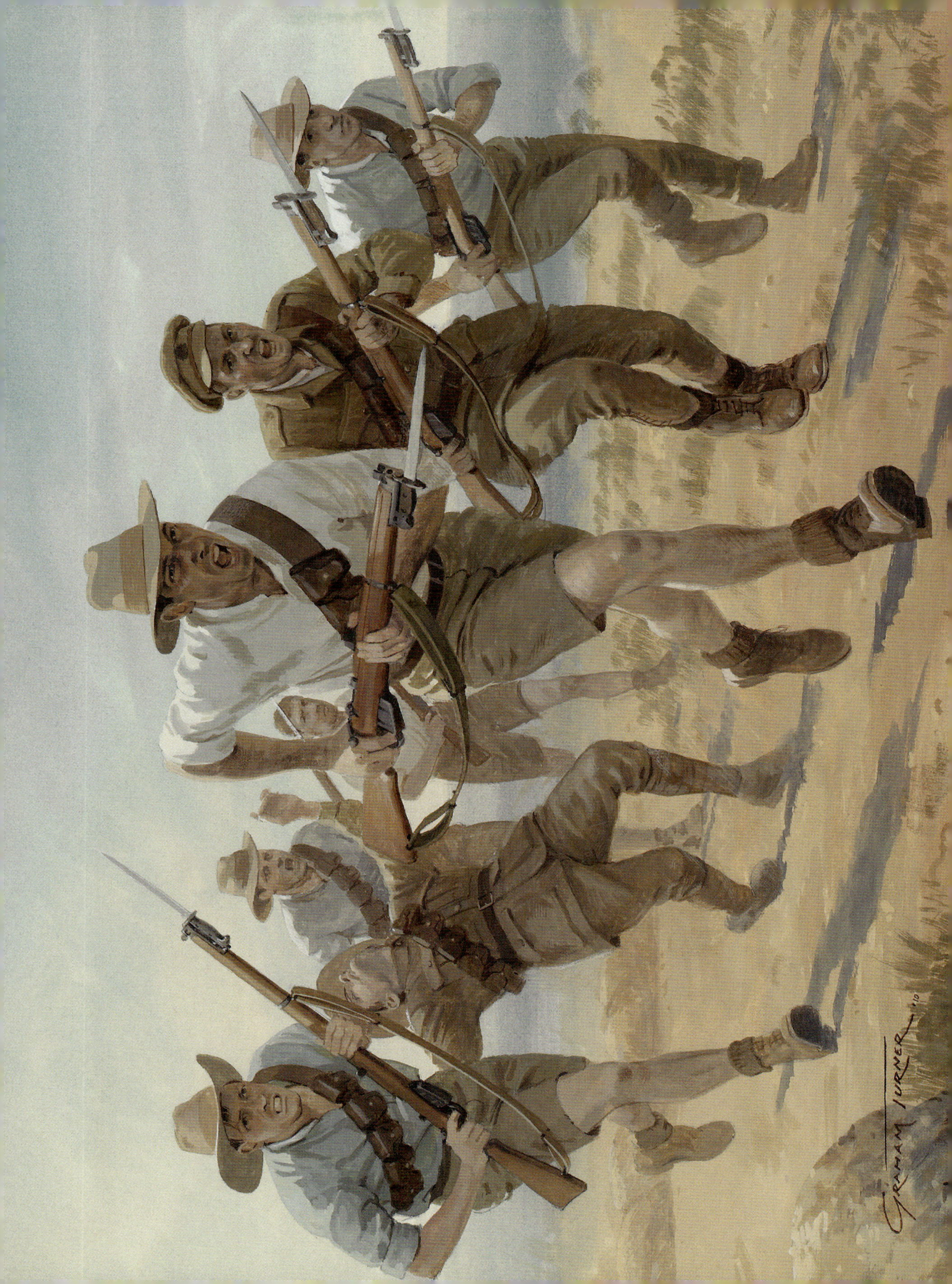

Wellington Mounted Rifles. 'Physical fear is a strange thing,' he decided. 'While all are more or less affected by it in a tight corner, most manage to contain it, but in some cases it causes them to lose all control over themselves.'

Some – like Private Frank McKenzie of the Auckland Battalion – claimed fear had little effect on them. 'Can tell you one feels a big fellow in a bayonet charge, with a few bombs in his belt and ten deaths in his rifle,' confessed McKenzie. 'It is the best and most exciting feeling I've ever had. The old primeval instincts and blood lust are only thinly buried after all.' Lance Corporal W. Francis was cut from the same cloth. 'Up the hill ... we swarm,' he later recounted, contrasting his training with the reality of combat, 'the lust to kill is on us, we see red ... they run, we after them, no thrust one and parry, in goes the bayonet the handiest way.'

Others thought very differently. One member of 8th Light Horse had no time for would-be soldiers. 'You ... always hear people say that they would like to be in a bayonet charge,' he told his sister, 'but the bayonet charges of previous wars are absolutely child's play compared to present methods and the person who says he likes them is fit for the asylum.'

New South Welshman Private Reginald Donkin served with 1st Battalion and survived the landing on 25 April. 'I know it is right and proper that a man should go back and fight again,' he later wrote in his diary, 'but Sunday's battle and the horror of the trenches Sunday night ... have unnerved me completely.' A month later he was wondering what happened to the rest of his 13 mates: 'myself I consider lucky getting away from the acres of dead men... And now I go back there... God only knows what is in store for me.' Donkin was killed on 15 August; his name is recorded on the Lone Pine Memorial.

Few Turkish prisoners were taken at the start of the campaign; accusations that the enemy had attacked while waving white flags, and rumours – never substantiated – of mutilation of the dead both had their effect. Sergeant Humphrey Macarty of 10th Battalion came across a soldier guarding eight wounded Turks. 'I am only going to bandage them up,' he told Macarty,

The ramshackle nature of the accommodation available for soldiers, and for brigade and divisional headquarters staff, is apparent here. One of General Hamilton's staff officers described the situation thus: 'The place is in perpetual motion like an antheap of khaki ants. It is almost inconceivable that a whole Army Corps, headquarters and all, should be holding such a position, the whole exposed to shellfire'. (Liddle Collection)

The truce of 24 May. Many witnesses found it hard to get used to the absence of noise: one Anzac thought it 'seemed very queer all day with everything so quiet… Our men and the Turks were exchanging cigarettes.' (Liddle Collection)

placing his prisoners in a row. But Macarty remained unconvinced by this apparent act of charity: 'Finis Turk,' he concluded. However, as the summer wore on, the men of Anzac developed a grudging regard for their foes. They looked on 'Abdul', 'Johnny' or 'Jack' Turk as a tough opponent, but for the most part a fair one.

A truce called on 24 May enabled both sides to collect and bury their dead. A member of one of the burial parties was shocked by the 'strange effect of the silence'. 'I found a sort of "hurting" of the ears,' he reported, 'obviously caused by the sudden cessation of heavy, continuous fire that, from the time of the Landing, had never ceased for a moment. It was an amazing sensation – nearly as great as the sudden realization that for a few hours a man was safe!'

At 1545hrs both sides returned to their positions ready to resume hostilities. 'At 4.30, as punctual as possible,' continued George Grove, 'shots were exchanged between us and the enemy. [However] no very heavy firing was experienced until 3.00 a.m.' This brief period of respite was the first of several; later in the campaign other unofficial truces were arranged for the same purpose at different places along the line.

According to the original caption, this narrow trench in the New Zealand section was only 14m from the Turkish lines. Yet, like all trenches, it was still kept scrupulously clean, with the aim of reducing disease. (Suzanne Duncan Collection, Turnbull Library)

ON THE BEACHHEAD

So heavy were the losses experienced during the first month of the campaign that the Anzacs soon needed reinforcement, and the light horse and Mounted Rifles regiments arrived from Egypt on 12 May to fight as infantry. The hard-pressed infantrymen enjoyed watching their equestrian comrades 'sweating up and down hill under the weight of an infantry pack.' And there was plenty of banter too. 'Our fellows chaff them a lot and are always ragging them about their horses,' confessed Clutha McKenzie. Comments like 'Where are your spurs?' or 'What ho! The elite without their nags!' followed them around.

Quinn's Post, slightly in advance of the main line of trenches, was the 'key to the whole position'. As Major-General Godley described it, 'There was no back to the Australian trenches, just the cliff.' The Anzac and Turkish lines here were only a matter of metres apart.
(Liddle Collection)

'We are all as lousy as a bandicoot … the vermin are a dam [sic] sight worse than the Turks to fight,' wrote one exasperated soldier. Hunting for lice was a daily chore; they even got into the food rations.
(Liddle Collection)

Once the stalemate was established men spent 48 hours in the trenches, followed by 48 hours out. 'We are glad of the spells', admitted Major Eric Brind of 23rd Battalion. 'It is of course a big strain while we are in and every day we have some casualties, as … bombs continually fly over both ways.' The commanding officer of the relieving Wellingtons described how a tour at Quinn's Post had affected his comrades in the Auckland and Canterbury Battalions. They set off 'as though they were leaving a death trap. They were cowed and dreaded being in the position.' An issue of rum doled out just before going into rest (rather than before an attack as became British practice) sealed the duty tour for many. 'It puts a different aspect on life altogether,' said one grateful recipient, 'and you see smiles where before only gloom reigned.'

Lieutenant-Colonel Percy Fenwick, a New Zealand medical officer, had to adjust to a new way of life on the beachhead. 'We live so much under the shadow of sudden death, that one sees things very differently to ordinary times,' he concluded. 'Life is normally complicated, here it is savagely simple. Eat while you can, help all you can, sleep when and where you can, and above all, grin and keep a stiff upper lip. Even a mechanical smile is better than an anxious look. Worrying is not good for the men.'

'You were dead from the feet up,' declared Sergeant Harvey Johns of the Wellingtons, 'and at night time when you were standing to, you would sell your soul for an hour's sleep.' One man did succumb; Private John Dunn of the Wellingtons was condemned to death in July for falling asleep at his post – the only New Zealander handed a capital sentence during the campaign. Dunn had not been relieved from sentry duty at the proper time and thus the sentence was later remitted. But his reprieve was only temporary; little more than a week later he was dead – killed in action at Chunuk Bair.

The beach at Anzac Cove. The beach itself was extremely narrow and was used primarily for stores. Most stores came ashore on North Beach. This was more open, making it easier to move around, but also more vulnerable to Turkish fire. (Liddle Collection)

No Australian soldier was condemned to death during the Gallipoli campaign. The 1903 Defence Act listed only two capital crimes – mutiny and desertion. And any death sentence required further ratification by the Governor General, a political impossibility. Australian commanders on the Western Front would later lobby (unsuccessfully) for the Act to be amended.

The Turkish trenches were scarcely more spacious than those on the Anzac side. Here, Australians have taken possession of some Turkish trenches at Lone Pine. (Liddle Collection)

Relief from the front-line trenches brought no end to a soldier's troubles. Private Hartley Palmer of the Canterbury Battalion summed up life behind the lines: 'if you laid down in the dust you got full of lice, and annoyed by flies and men walking over you'. Lice (known as 'chats' to the Anzacs) infested clothing, and hunting them down (or 'chatting') was an everyday chore.

Flies were present in their millions, the product of summer heat, primitive sanitation and the proximity of the battlefield. Trooper Ion Idriess of 5th Light Horse was ambushed when he opened a tin of jam: 'the flies rushed [it] … all fighting amongst themselves. I wrapped my overcoat over the tin and gouged [them] out … then spread the biscuit, then held my hand over it and drew the biscuit out of the coat. But a lot of flies flew into my mouth and beat about inside … I nearly howled with rage … Of all the b*****ds of places this is the greatest b******d in the world.'

Food was relatively plentiful. Rice, biscuits, cheese, bully beef and jam were all available, and sometimes there was bacon for breakfast. Bread was a luxury seen by few until early June, when 1st Australian Field Bakery moved from Lemnos to the island of Imbros, only 24 kilometres offshore. Between 13 June and the end of July, when British units arrived to join it, the bakery shipped 14,500 bread rations daily. Although the bread got a bit wet from travelling on an open trawler it was still considered preferable to the standard-issue hard biscuit (or 'Anzac wafer').

Captain Joseph Beeston, commanding 4th Australian Field Ambulance at the beachhead, took a positive view of the rations provided:

> stacks of biscuits, cheese and preserved beef, all of the best. One particular kind of biscuit, known as the 'forty-niner,' had forty-nine holes in it, was believed to take forty-nine years to bake, and needed forty-nine chews to a bite. But there were also beautiful hams and preserved vegetables, and with these and a tube of Oxo a very palatable soup could be prepared. A well-known firm in England puts up a tin which they term an Army Ration, consisting of meat and vegetables, nicely seasoned and very palatable.

Private Victor Worland, serving with 2nd Australian Field Ambulance, agreed: he was, he reckoned, 'getting excellent tucker'.

But, as time passed, opinions began to change. 'For a time this ration was eagerly looked for and appreciated,' noted Captain Beeston, 'but later on, when the men began to get stale, it did not agree with them so well; it appeared to be too rich for many of us.'

The basic Anzac diet was at best unvarying and monotonous, although extra treats were available from enterprising sailors selling milk, eggs, tea or chocolate on the beach. Prices were high but many Anzacs felt they were worth paying just 'to get a change'. The diet was also deficient in two essential vitamins, B1 and C, leading to a number of cases of beriberi and scurvy. Most seriously of all, the food provided was ill-adapted to the Turkish climate. In the scorching summer heat, bully beef could almost be poured from the tin, while the hard tack was rock hard. Gordon Kilner, serving with the Light Horse Field Ambulance, lost five teeth in a struggle with some of these biscuits.

Talk inevitably turned to memories of home; but not everyone wanted to reminisce. 'I smacked a chap in the eye tonight for talking about steak and eggs,' confessed Douglas Argyle. 'Carrying tea from the cookhouse to the trenches up a steep hill,' was another chore. 'Men over here do the work that a horse does at home,' he complained.

Free cigarettes were distributed to the troops. Sergeant Ditmer of the Auckland Battalion thought the first issue of 'Major Drapkins', 'the best of all issues to be received on the Peninsula'. However, their successors made a less favourable impression: 'Of later issues … "Rough Riders" and "Carrolls" and "Silk Cut" were surplus stock manufactured for the South African War – and they tasted like it.' Luckiest of all were the soldiers who received parcels from home, filled with sweets, cigarettes or socks. But everyone got a special present in December – the Christmas billy, a small metal container filled with treats, sent by civilians back home. 'Could the people of Australia but have seen the happy results of their thoughtful kindness,' wrote Captain Frank Coen of 18th Battalion, 'their own Xmas would indeed have been happy.'

Williams Pier, North Beach, was named after Brigadier-General Godfrey Williams, the Anzac Chief Engineer. This was the longer of the two piers built here, and even survived the great storm of 8 November unscathed. A tramway was laid in September 1915 to move heavy stores. An old freighter, the Milo, *was eventually sunk at the end of the pier to provide shelter for the cargo barges. (Liddle Collection)*

Providing an adequate supply of water to the troops in the beachhead was a constant problem. Here, at the foot of Walker's Ridge, men come to collect their ration from water tanks dragged up from the beach. (Preece Family Collection, Turnbull Library)

The impending evacuation brought unexpected bounty. Heading down to Rest Gully on 15 December, Edgar Worrall of 24th Battalion was delighted by the sight confronting him: 'Things are being given away wholesale. Uniforms, tobacco and food of every description. Feasted on strawberries and cream (canned), fruit salad and stewed fruit, fish, tomatoes, jams of the choicest brands, butter and well – it would take a cook to mention it all. I scarcely remember ever feeding so well in my life. All stores given away, ready for evacuation.' Private C. J. Walsh of the Canterbury Battalion also had a red-letter day to record in his diary: 'Saturday 11 December 1915: Got first butter issue since leaving Egypt.'

Water was scarce throughout the operation. The divisional engineers landed close on the heels of the infantry at Anzac Cove, with orders to bore for water as close as possible to the front lines. They managed to find some springs, but these were never sufficient to provide an ample supply for the troops. At best they produced only some 90,000 litres of water per day, and during the summer months they started to dry up. Field Service Regulations recommended

A hectic scene as stores are landed. The barges have to come close inshore to discharge their cargo, making them vulnerable to Turkish shellfire. (Liddle Collection)

Sea bathing off Anzac Beach. Tied up to the piers are some of the boats that plied between the beach and the transports standing offshore. (Liddle Collection)

4.5 litres of water per man per day – but this target was never met. Each man on the peninsula was allowed just one pint (0.57 litres) a day for all his washing and shaving needs. George Grove and his comrades in 2nd Field Company had to mount guard over a well to ensure that the precious liquid was distributed fairly – not only to the carts used to supply the infantry, but also to the animals of the Indian Mule Corps and the Zion Mule Corps.

'The actual fighting at Anzac was easiest of all' concluded Charles Saunders of the New Zealand Engineers. 'The fatigue work was enormous, colossal. Imagine a man with two kerosene tins full of water tied together with a belt and slung over the shoulder climbing for half a mile up these grades, slipping back, up and on again, the heat of the sun terrible, bullets and shells everywhere, and, as often happened, a bullet and shrapnel hitting the tin and bursting it and the priceless fluid running away just as he had scrambled almost to the top. Nothing for it but to go all the way down again for some more.'

Despite the dangers of Turkish shellfire and snipers, sea bathing was the only way of keeping clean. Charles Saunders relished the opportunity for a dip. 'We had our swim during the afternoon and how we did enjoy it,' he confessed. 'It is a rather weird experience swimming with the shrapnel bursting all around one, and yet one would rather do that than go without the only means of getting a wash.' James Hutchison, serving with the New Zealand Artillery, took a wry view of the scene: 'On any afternoon the beach looks just like a holiday resort except that bathing suits are not the fashion.'

Corporal Frank Ponting of 4th Battalion had a lucky escape when he and his mates went down to the water's edge one day: 'After swimming, we sat on one of the barges to get dressed. I had puttees and [my friend] Chalker had slacks so he was dressed before me and while waiting walked away and rolled me a cigarette. I went over to get the cigarette when Whiz! Bang! a shell from Beachy Bill burst on the place I'd been sitting ten seconds before.'

As shortages and material privations took their toll, soldiers in the front line began to vent their rage on their senior commanders. Sergeant John Skinner of the Otago Battalion took a scathing view of the New Zealand GOC (general officer commanding), Major-General Godley. A former British regular officer, Godley had never made much effort to win the affections of his men: '[he] never said "gidday boys" to us or anything else or asked how far away the Turk was or asked for a periscope to look over the top... I thought it was a pretty poor performance.' The 'bludgers' on the beach became the scapegoat for all the ills of the Anzac Corps. Nor were the bludgers confined to just the beach. 'A bomb woodened 13 of our fellows one day,' noted Clutha McKenzie, 'including one of our officers, who however was incapable, and makes way for a better man'.

At regimental level things were rather different. Here, the shared experience of danger – battalion headquarters were often little more than 50m from the front line – brought junior officers and their men together, making the dividing line between them much less pronounced than in the contemporary British Army. Birdwood, too, escaped much of the censure: Private Benjamin Smart of the Wellingtons reckoned the commander of the Anzac Corps 'a real decent soldier', liked by all.

However, the British in general formed the butt of many derogatory comments. The Anzacs had gone into the conflict with high expectations of the forces which created the British Empire. But the soldiers they encountered in British Territorial and Service battalions came as a shock. They were scarcely better trained than the Anzacs themselves – little more than civilians, shorter in stature, and with no sort of monopoly on military competence. 'I don't go much on the Naval Division,' commented New Zealand Engineer Wallace Saunders, '[because] several have shot their toes off cleaning their rifles.'

One officer in the Canterbury Battalion had considered the Royal Marine Light Infantry, 'the smartest and finest infantry in [the] world' – until, that is, he met them in the field. Reports of British troops panicking under fire on 10 August during the Turkish attack on Chunuk Bair did little to assist mutual understanding. 'The Tommies here,' reported Sergeant Edney Moore of the Medical Corps, 'are not making a good impression on Australians and there is no doubt they are not the same stamp of fellows as the Australians and New Zealanders. They haven't the stamina … and they certainly won't or can't fight like our fellows.'

Many British officers gave the impression that 'regular' soldiers would have found the task facing the Anzacs much easier to accomplish. This type of attitude was bitterly resented by the Antipodeans, who saw little evidence to back up the notion. Like many others, Private Stanley Natusch of the Canterburys had gone to war thinking himself a soldier of the British Empire.

The cookhouse of 5th Light Horse in Wright's Gully. Meat hanging out in the open, as here, was prey to flies coming direct from the open latrines. In such conditions, it is hardly surprising that many of the Anzacs suffered from gastric complaints. At first, men simply catered for themselves and their mates; standards improved once more centralized arrangements had been put in place. (Liddle Collection)

'The days and nights continue to be gorgeous,' wrote one man on 11 November. But the weather changed quickly. On 26 November it snowed for three days, a novelty for many Anzacs, most of whom had never seen snow before. (Liddle Collection)

But Gallipoli changed his mind. He reckoned that 100,000 Australasians, led by 'our own officers', would have defeated the Turks by August.

However, Lord Kitchener, like Birdwood, attracted grudging respect, albeit of a distinctively Anzac kind. When Kitchener visited the peninsula in November he was quickly surrounded, 'by a crowd of privates, none of them in the correct military posture, hands in their pockets, commenting freely to their mates, moving only just sufficiently to allow the exalted one to make slow progress, and taking snaps of him under his very nose. Yet in a strange way there was no disrespect. The same men back at home at an agricultural show would have gathered round a super bull and discussed his points admiringly in much the same fashion.'

October and November brought storms, biting winds and increasing cold, and many grew apprehensive about the coming winter. The October weather had made George Bollinger think of home. 'This morning was very bitter and reminded me of New Plymouth,' he wrote. But by November things were much worse: 'The air this morning was thin, very thin. The last 18 months our blood has got very thin and we feel the cold.' The first snowfall at the end of that month was no cause for celebration. According to Bollinger, there was 'no inclination amongst the men to go snowballing. We were miserable. Perhaps it is well this has set in so early as it gives fair warning as to what we have to provide against.'

Yet when the Anzacs finally received the order to evacuate it produced mixed emotions. Many were reluctant to abandon a job half done and still more to leave the graves of their comrades unattended. Edgar Worrall (24th Battalion) volunteered to join the small party which would stay behind to fight the rearguard action. 'It will be a serious business and we will be very lucky if we ever reach the beach and boats,' he confided to his diary. 'But at school I learnt this motto: "Dulce et decorum est pro patria mori" and I feel composed, and, if possible, happy. One thing hurts above all others – the graves of fallen heroes, friends and fellow schoolmates must be left to be overrun by Abdul. Perhaps the sentiment is foolish but nevertheless it is there.'

One New Zealander, quoted in conversation with Lieutenant-Colonel Hart of the Wellingtons, spoke for many of his compatriots: 'Well sir, I hope our poor pals who lie all around us sleep soundly, and do not stir in discontent as we go filing away from them forever.'

OUT OF ACTION

In the initial rush to fill out the ranks of the first Anzac battalions, pre-existing medical complaints were often ignored. Many men were hospitalized shortly after their arrival in Egypt, unable to withstand the rigours of the training regime imposed upon them. Infectious diseases such as measles were rife, while venereal disease posed another problem, incapacitating 3 per cent of the total force. A special hospital was set up in Abbassia (Cairo) to deal with venereal cases, and as many as 1,350 men were sent home, and eventually discharged, for this reason.

Once the fighting started, the Anzacs sustained heavy losses and continued to do so throughout the campaign. A total of 16,000 men were put ashore on 25 April, and by the end of that first day alone some 2,000 had become casualties. One week into the fight and 1st Division had lost about half its effectives. Hardest hit was 3rd Brigade, reduced to one quarter of its strength after just three days of combat. By August, 15th Battalion, serving with the Australian and New Zealand Division, could muster only 170 of the 959 men who had landed in April; the survivors were 'thin, haggard, as weak as kittens and covered with suppurating sores'. Private Errol Devlin had served in New Guinea before transferring to 18th Battalion. He thought the wounded were the lucky ones. 'It is quite common for men to go mad here,' he added. 'The strain on the nerves is so severe.'

Amongst the New Zealanders, the Otago Battalion suffered particularly badly. It was destroyed as an effective combat unit by its unsuccessful attempt to capture Baby 700 in May. Four months later, its North Otago Company contained just 18 men commanded by two lance corporals. Even in 1916, the arrival of the men of 8th Reinforcements could bring the battalion up to only one-third of its normal complement. By August, almost all the members of the original New Zealand contingent had become casualties, their gallantry unable to compensate for poor staff work.

Stretcher-bearers evacuate the wounded. The medical facilities on the beach, even to their commander, were, 'a hideous nightmare… I shall never forget the incessant stream of wounded, [and] the courage … of the men.' (Price Collection, Turnbull Library)

Some 50,000 Australians were engaged at Gallipoli. Of this total, 28,150 became casualties during the course of the campaign, including 8,709 who lost their lives. So many men died in hard-to-reach places, or within the Turkish lines, that 61 per cent have no known grave. As far as the New Zealand Expeditionary Force is concerned, the official history of World War I, Fred Waite's *The New Zealanders at Gallipoli*, gave a figure of 7,571 casualties from the 8,556 men who served there. Of these, 2,701 were killed in action, died of their wounds or died from disease. However, a second New Zealand figure, given in the New Zealand Expeditionary Force roll of honour and taken as correct by modern scholars, amends this total to 2,721 (and, like the Australians, 61 per cent have no known grave).

Proper lines of evacuation were established only as the campaign progressed. Australia eventually provided three General Hospitals, all capable of accommodating up to 520 beds. Two had arrived in Egypt in January – No. 1 Hospital was located at the Heliopolis Palace Hotel on the north-east outskirts of Cairo, and No. 2 Hospital at Mena – but No. 3 Hospital did not reach Lemnos until August. The most seriously wounded were evacuated again, some to Malta and others as far as the UK. A patriotic Australian had set aside Harefield Park, in Middlesex, as a convalescent home for wounded servicemen, but it was later converted to a 500-bed hospital. By September, more New Zealanders were recovering in England (2,927) than were serving on the peninsula itself (2,840).

The three General Hospitals were supplemented by two Stationary Hospitals (one on Lemnos and, by November, another on North Beach), a Casualty Clearing Station and Field Ambulance units. Also accompanying the landing forces were three transport vessels employed as hospital ships: the *Gascon* had room for up to 300 serious cases, while the *Clan MacGillivray* and the *Seang Choon* were intended for lighter cases.

The number of casualties incurred during the initial invasion overwhelmed the inadequate medical facilities. Hamilton had based his plan around a rapid advance inland, allowing the lightly wounded to be treated at the beach, while more serious cases were evacuated to the transports standing offshore. But, with no room on the narrow beach for the medical units, everyone had to go offshore. Chaos reigned. Crammed into lighters, the first casualties did not sail from Anzac Cove until the evening of 26 April, and the transports were soon overwhelmed.

Wounded men are loaded onto a hospital barge, which will ferry them to a waiting ship. Lack of foresight and planning meant that there were not enough ships available to transport the wounded – particularly in the early days – and many died who might otherwise have been saved. (Liddle Collection)

G. CASUALTIES ARRIVING AT LEMNOS

The Australian Army Nursing Service was originally formed as part of the New South Wales state forces and became a national service following confederation. The indoor uniform adopted was similar to that worn by the British Queen Alexandra's Imperial Military Nursing Service, but with the addition of a cloth arm badge, and brass 'Australia' shoulder titles worn on the scarlet tippet. Service dress consisted of a grey jacket with chocolate-brown shoulder straps, a grey full-length skirt and a grey hat with a chocolate-brown band.

Nurses served on board some of the vessels acting as hospital ships as well as in the hospital on Lemnos, which had a staff of 69 nurses. On board the *Sicilia*, Lydia King was rushed off her feet: 'I shall never forget the awful feeling of hopelessness on night duty. It was dreadful. I had two wards downstairs, each over 100 patients and then I had small wards upstairs – altogether about 250 patients to look after, and one orderly and one Indian sweeper. Shall not describe their wounds, they were too awful. One loses sight of all the honour and the glory in the work we are doing.' Despite the conditions, Nellie Pike thought rather differently: 'We were all glad to be taking part in the great adventure. They were grim and tragic, but somehow inspiring days.'

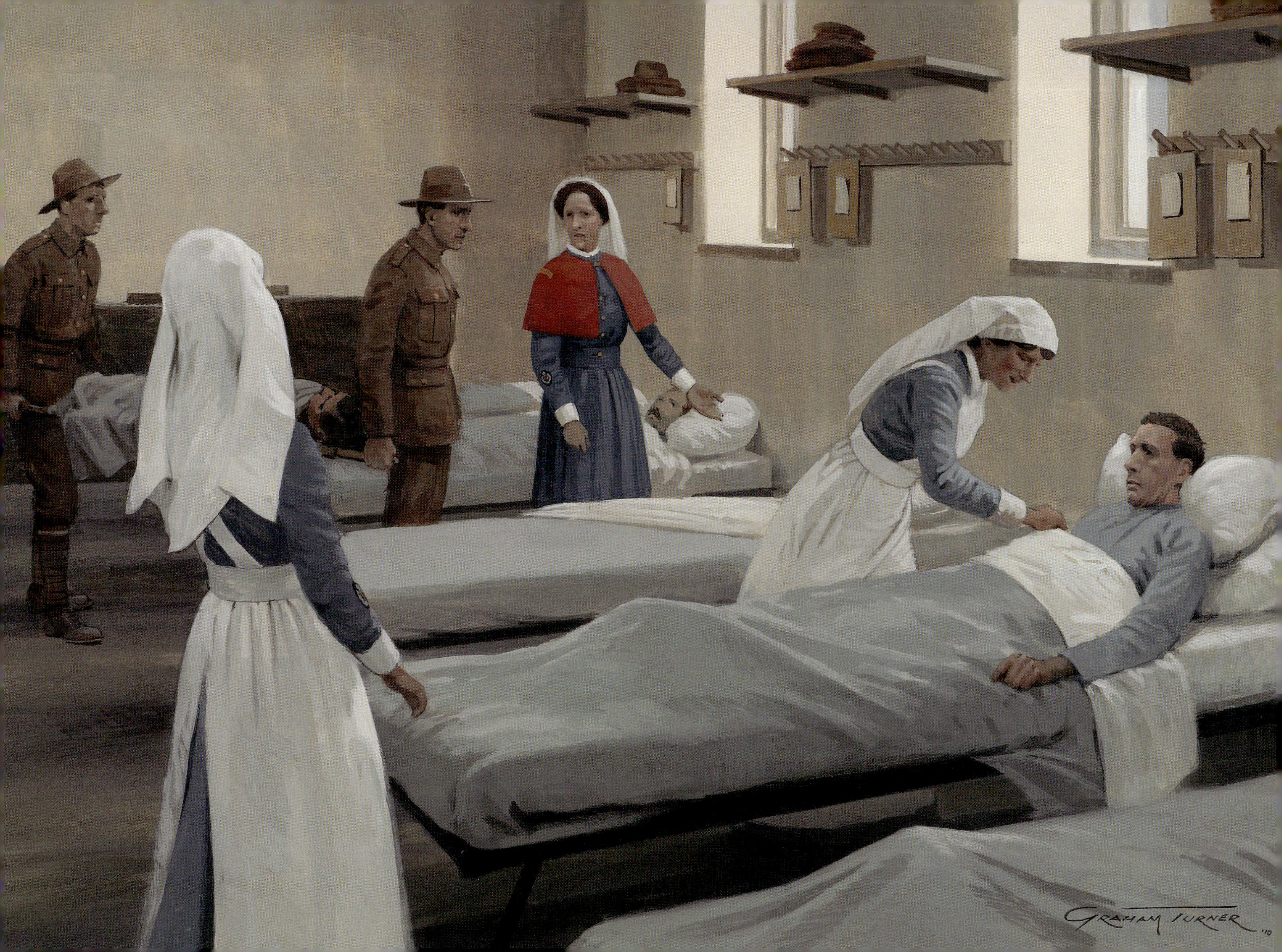
GRAHAM TURNER '10

Royal Navy midshipman (and later vice admiral) E. W. Longley-Cook was on board one of the lighters, carrying 'this load of wounded from ship to ship, only to be waved away as they were full.' In desperation, he eventually approached his own vessel, the *Prince of Wales*. 'Risking a beating for insolence,' he secured alongside and went up to the officer of the watch. '[I] told him what had happened and that *he must* take them. All was well, the wounded were taken on board and I returned to the beach.'

From Lemnos or Imbros, the first wave of casualties continued on to Alexandria, 1,140km away, many travelling in ships only recently used to transport horses and mules, and not yet cleaned down in preparation for their new role. Within a few days, the two Australian hospitals in Cairo were inundated, and an auxiliary facility was set up at Luna Park, a former skating rink in the city. Lady Godley, wife of the New Zealand GOC, had never seen such pandemonium: 'Seven hundred beds in the awful heat and the tin roof. All the patients seem cheery, but how anyone can get well in such a place is past belief.' For Isaac Unsworth, a volunteer with the Australian Salvation Army, 'the sight of these 1,400 men lying there crowded together in this terrible heat with the flies pestering them was awful'. Controversy about the medical facilities in Egypt and the treatment they provided would continue to rumble on for the rest of the war and beyond.

Later attacks would also see many hours pass before casualties received adequate medical attention. Wherever possible, stretcher-bearers carried the wounded down the steep slopes to the beach. One unit, 3rd Field Ambulance, had landed with the first wave. 'We didn't carry arms,' recalled Jim McPhee, 'just water bottles and a big field dressing for shrapnel wounds, you couldn't manage any more by the time you got a weight on a stretcher… I remember we carried a little bundle of kindling wood on our backs that first day. The sailors had broken up cases and bundled the pieces for us so we could boil a billy.'

But it was impossible to reach all the casualties. Signaller Robert Kenny recalled the fate of one man stranded in a gully in front of positions occupied by 4th Battalion. Somewhere down there a wounded Australian cried out, 'Water! Water! For God's sake cobbers bring me water… Don't let a man stay here!' Kenny and his mates volunteered to go to him; but permission was refused. 'Both sides were shooting at anyone in front of our trenches as being night friend could not be distinguished from foe. Towards morning, the cries ceased.'

The first batch of New Zealanders wounded in the attacks of 6 August wait patiently on the beach in full sun for evacuation. After the chaos of April, arrangements for the wounded did improve somewhat, but men continued to die on the beach through lack of medical attention. (Liddle Collection)

Wounded Anzacs recovering at Imtarfa Hospital, Malta. Conditions in the hospitals on Malta were much better than those in Cairo. (Liddle Collection)

Some of the casualties trapped in no man's land tried to make their own way to the shore; but few reached their goal. After the battles of early August, Sergeant Harold Jackson (13th Battalion) reported that, 'from the trench down to the beach, about 4 miles [6.4km], is one long line of grey stiff bodies of men who have died trying to get down to the beach unassisted'.

The journey down to Anzac Cove was hazardous for casualty and stretcher-bearer alike, but the beach itself was no sanctuary. It was always under fire and many of those waiting for treatment were wounded a second time by shrapnel. And shortages afflicted the medical units just as they did the infantry and artillery. Lieutenant-Colonel Percy Fenwick became fatalistic about the conditions he was forced to work in: 'This absent-minded war ... medical supplies not there "yet"... I would very much like to live long enough to hear the explanation, but I fear I will not do so.'

The Turks captured just 70 Australians and 25 New Zealanders during the course of the campaign – a relatively small number considering the nature of the fighting. This was not the Western Front, where the Allies were more inclined to leave the wounded to the mercies of the enemy; here, the Anzacs did their utmost to bring their casualties back into their lines. Captured officers were held in relative comfort and were paid a small allowance through the Red Cross. However, ordinary soldiers were forced to work on railway and road construction in exceptionally harsh conditions. Unsurprisingly, some prisoners lost their lives, either through accidents at work or disease (many were sent to areas of Turkey where malaria was prevalent). Official figures published after the war suggest that 30 per cent of all Australians in Turkish hands died while in captivity.

But the Turk was not the only enemy facing the Anzacs; illness posed just as great a threat. Only twice during the whole campaign – in May and during the August offensives – did the proportion of wounded men leaving the peninsula exceed that of those evacuated through illness. For every wounded man, another three or so were 'sick' – riven with dysentery, non-specific diarrhoea (the 'Turkey Trot') or enteric fever. Sergeant Joseph Gasparich of the

Canterbury Battalion was one such sufferer. Feeling as if 'my whole alimentary tract was on fire and was periodically being torn from me,' Gasparich was evacuated to Imbros. There he found himself 'housed in a great marquee with dozens of others in like state. We slept on the ground and were fed stew and tea which only made matters worse... Some men were so weak that they crawled to the latrines and stayed there until they died.'

During the first week of September 7.5 per cent of the troops on Anzac were evacuated, a significantly higher proportion than at Helles and Suvla. The Dardanelles Commission later sought an explanation. Much of the blame was attributed to the primitive sanitary arrangements. 'We had ordinary open latrines,' explained one New Zealand officer. 'The space in Monash Gully which was not under fire was very limited and it was very difficult getting sites for latrines.' With swarms of flies contaminating food, fierce heat, poor diet and dehydration, it is scarcely surprising that so many Anzacs fell ill. Only autumn brought relief, with cooler weather, more effective sanitary arrangements at the beachhead and less intense fighting all combining to reduce the burden on the over-stretched medical facilities.

AWAY FROM THE FRONT

The arrival of reinforcements evoked mixed feelings. Clutha McKenzie had no time for those who reached Gallipoli in May. 'The reinforcements have arrived and they sicken me,' he raged. 'There are none of our officers left to see about promotion for the survivors. F. H. J., who has another section now, gets no promotion while cowards who asked to be left at the base in Egypt and who have seen no fighting retain their rank.'

The arrival of 2nd Division in August was a different matter. Although, like veterans everywhere, the first contingent enjoyed watching new arrivals dodge shells and bullets, C. E. W. Bean claimed that the new men were like 'a fresh breeze from the outback'. According to one 1st Division veteran, the recent arrivals came straight from civilian life. They 'looked like a different race of men,' he said, 'and made us realize our wasted and worn-out condition'. The new men were equally shocked by the condition of their comrades on the beachhead, finding the troops there 'listless, weak, emaciated by dysentery, prematurely aged'.

Nevertheless rivalry between the two divisions was keen. Every soldier claimed his division as the home of 'dinkum' (genuine) Aussies, characterizing the other mob as 'adventurers'. The newcomers of 2nd Division stigmatized the men of 1st Division as 'six-bob-a-day' tourists, who signed up only to take part in the 'great adventure'. Far from it, replied the veterans. It was the men of the 2nd who were drawn by the idea of 'adventure', after reading about the landings in the newspapers.

H

REINFORCEMENTS ARRIVING AT ANZAC COVE

These men, newly arrived reinforcements, wear the peaked forage cap, bound with leather on the peak. Although it consumed fewer resources than the bush hat, it did not offer as much protection from the sun, so a cotton neckcloth was issued as well. The men continued to wear the cap after the landing, although many chose to wear the bush hat whenever they could. On their jackets they wear the arm patch of 5th Battalion, the red lower segment indicating a battalion from Victoria.

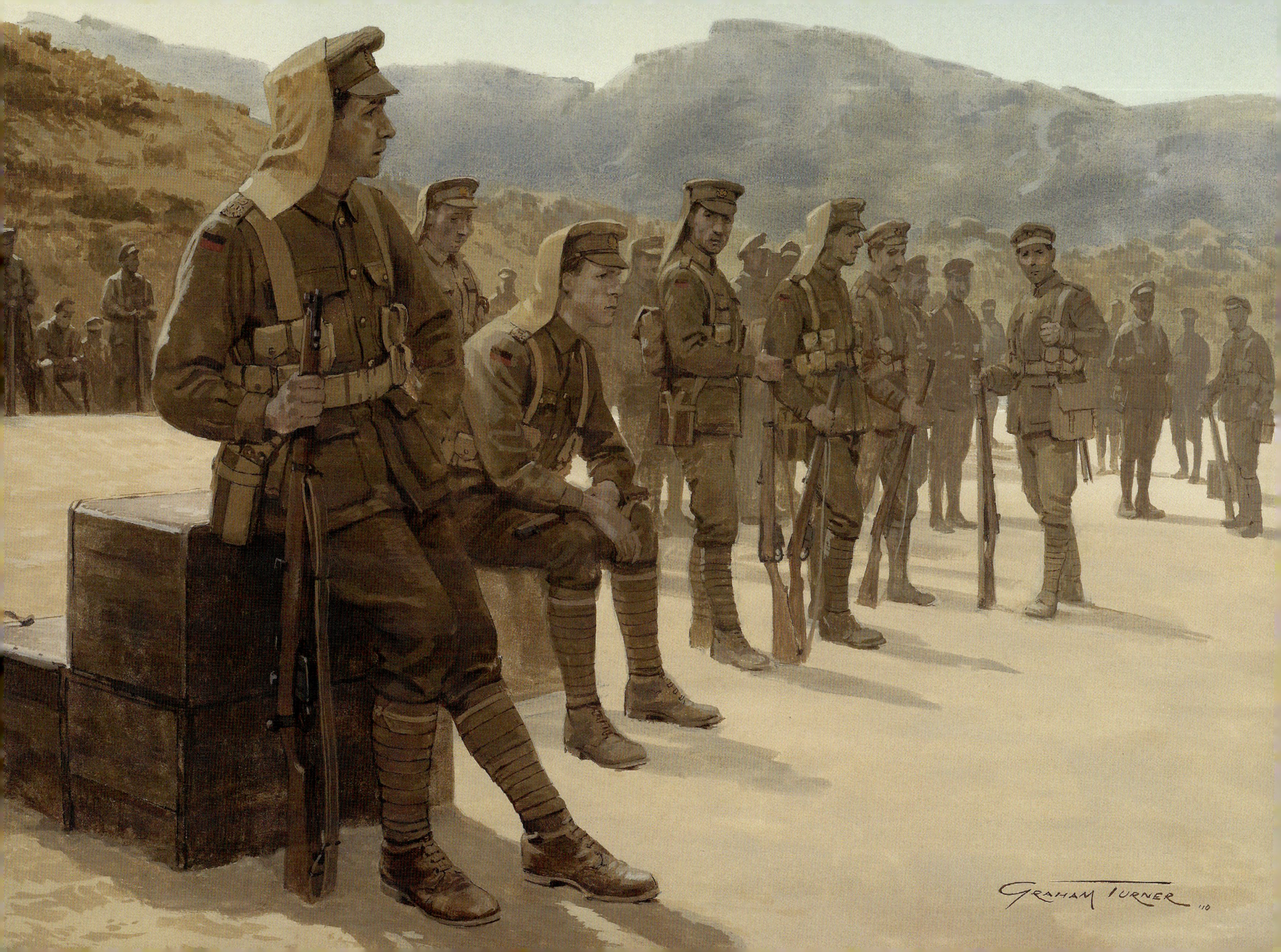
GRAHAM TURNER '10

New Zealanders snatch a game of cards in the trenches. Lack of space and the constant shelling gave little opportunity for recreation on the beachhead, although card and two-up 'schools' flourished. (Judge Gresson Collection, Turnbull Library)

The men who landed on 25 April had little chance to escape the peninsula until the arrival of 2nd Division. A schedule was drawn up allowing each unit to spend some time at Sarpi Rest Camp on Lemnos. Private James Fitzmaurice of 10th Light Horse arrived on the island on 10 November. At first he found it difficult to adjust: 'Feel as if we are in a new world. Cannot sleep at night as there is no noise.' But later, his spirits restored after five weeks away from the peninsula, he pronounced himself 'as fit as a fiddle'. This was no holiday for the troops: drills, bomb-throwing training and route marches all kept them occupied. But the route marches were mercifully short in length, and there was plenty of opportunity for sport, as well as horse- and donkey-riding. More significantly, the troops ate better and received a daily issue of beer. Many suffered from stomach upsets at first, finding it difficult to adjust to the richer diet; but in the long term it significantly improved their health.

Lance Corporal Archibald Barwick of 1st Battalion spent one day helping 'to run up a thumping big marquee for the YMCA'. He thought the YMCA a splendid institution:

> they have stuck to us through thick and thin. At Lemnos they not only supplied us with pens, ink, writing paper etc, but ran a piano as well besides a gramophone and supplied us with cricket sets, boxing gloves, draughts, chess, cards, quoits, footballs and 'goodness' only knows what else. The piano was a Godsend and it used to make the place quite merry of a night. The Greek children would stand with their mouth wide open and gaze at the gramophone while it was playing as if it was some marvellous thing. I suppose it was to them the first one they had ever seen or heard.

But eventually the soldiers had to return to Gallipoli. Anne Donnell, a nursing sister, served on Lemnos with No. 3 Hospital. 'This morning we heard the band playing,' she wrote in her diary for 26 October. 'It was the 1st Brigade on its way back to Anzac after a rest. They came along the main street of our Hospital. We Sisters gather up all the cigarettes and chocolates and tins of food we can and throw them to the smiling faces as they march by. They are brave and apparently cheerful, though we all know how in their inner heart they dislike going back to all they remember there. It makes us feel terribly sad.'

The Australian Government decided at the outset to pay the men of the AIF a wage comparable to the average earnings of the working man at home. They settled on a figure of six shillings a day for a man holding the rank of private, of which one shilling was deferred until discharge. This made the Australian soldier the best paid of any during the war (five shillings equals approximately £11 at 2010 values). New Zealanders received five shillings in total, whereas the British were paid only one shilling. Many of the Australian troops were grateful for the money. 'I don't know about succeeding contingents,' wrote one of the first to set sail, 'but in this one there are many men to whom this was a real Godsend, men who've never been better dressed nor earned so much money before in their life.'

The original members of the AIF received no separation allowance and were obliged to allocate two shillings a day to their families (the New Zealanders had to allocate over three shillings). An allowance was eventually introduced in 1915, but on a restricted basis. It went only to those receiving less than eight (later ten) shillings a day, effectively limiting it to privates and junior NCOs.

Egypt provided the Anzacs with plenty of opportunities to spend their new-found wealth. The baser pleasures of the Haret el Wasser, the red-light district of Cairo, commonly known as 'The Wazzer', were not to everyone's taste. Some were drawn instead by history and culture, taking time to visit the museums and the nearby Pyramids. 'Cairo at night held no attraction [for me]' confessed Private Alexander Aitken of the Otago Battalion. 'I preferred to practice on the violin.' (This violin led a chequered existence. Accompanying its owner to Gallipoli and France, it was twice lost and recovered before ending its days behind glass at his old school.)

Aitken was not the only member of the Anzac Corps who failed to live up the stereotype of the Antipodean larrikin. Corporal Tom Louch of 11th Battalion was particularly shocked by the language of his British comrades-in-arms in and around Cairo. 'What really staggered us about the Tommies was their vocabulary,' he claimed. 'One four-letter word with variations provided nouns, verbs and adjectives – the staple of their conversation. The men in my section were not particularly straight-laced but they only swore in a mild way when exasperated.'

News from home was vitally important to those at the front. Here, a large heap of mail sacks at the beachhead await distribution to units, using the mules on the left of the picture. (Liddle Collection)

The aftermath of the 'Battle of the Wazzer', April 1915. The remains of a pile of bedding and clothing lie in the street after Anzac soldiers set them alight following an argument with a prostitute. (E. B. Paterson Collection, Turnbull Library)

The camps too laid on all kinds of recreation for the men: concerts, tennis, boxing and rugby – league and union (allowing Queensland and New South Wales, and the New Zealand provinces, to resume their traditional rivalries). Polo and a gymkhana were provided for lovers of equestrian sports – although participants had to make do with donkeys as mounts. Church parade was 'the least popular; it was held out in the desert where there wasn't a vestige of shade'. Inspections by senior officers were another inevitable feature of camp life: 'We marched as uprightly as the soft going would allow, mounted our fiercest touch-me-if-you-dare look, and as the chaps actually in range of the camera averaged over six feet in height right through, I guess we looked some fighting men, and no error.'

Another common pastime, which often goes unrecorded, was the game of 'two-up'. This form of gambling was illegal until 1989, when Australia finally relaxed the laws that banned it. Since then the game has been permitted only on Anzac Day, on the grounds that it forms part of the country's national heritage. The usual rules of two-up are relatively straightforward. The 'ringkeeper' controls the 'spinner' and the conduct of the game. The 'spinner' places two pennies on the 'kip' (a narrow strip of wood) and tosses them. To constitute a valid toss, the coins must reach at least two metres above the head of the spinner, they must not come into contact with any object or person, and they must land within the boundaries of the 'ring'. Players bet on two possible outcomes: either two heads or two tails appearing uppermost when the pennies land. No other result is valid. On Imbros, where two-up 'schools' flourished, one lucky nurse won over £70 (approximately £3,000 at 2010 values).

One of the more unsavoury episodes of the Anzac stay in Egypt, the so-called 'Battle of the Wazzer' took place on Good Friday 1915, shortly before the Corps left for Gallipoli. Feeling cheated by a prostitute, a group of Australians took their revenge by throwing furniture out into the street and setting fire to it. Unable to disperse the rioters, the provost guard resorted to firing shots into the crowd, and an armed picquet was eventually needed to clear the streets. Alfred Clennett, a sergeant serving with 9th Battery, Australian Field Artillery, was worried about the reputation of the Anzac Corps, but he nevertheless offered a plea in mitigation: 'It is a great pity it happened. It will get us a bad name all over the world. [The men] have been bottled up here so long and were rather excited at the prospect of getting away, still that does not excuse them.'

Larrikin behaviour of this kind certainly became part of the Anzac legend: 'The wild Colonial Corps has left Cairo,' remarked a senior British officer on their departure from the city. And a second 'Battle of the Wazzer' took place on 30 July, when men from 2nd Division followed the example of their predecessors. Yet the misdeeds of the few should not be allowed to characterize the Corps as a whole. The majority of men behaved well while on campaign, and their relationships with women at home and abroad were entirely conventional for the time.

ANZAC

The conduct of operations on the peninsula continues to provoke lively debate, but the significance of the landings in establishing and developing Australia and New Zealand as separate nations, rather than mere adjuncts of the mother country, is undeniable.

Initial reactions back home to the Gallipoli landings were muted. Official censorship combined with a perception that the 'real war' was taking place in France to downplay events. The *Sydney Morning Herald* felt obliged to reassure its readers that 'they need not admit that the services of the Australians in Turkey are less worthy in the history of the war'. Accolades were later heaped upon the Anzacs from many quarters, official and unofficial, both during and after the campaign. In his one-volume history of Australia's war, *Anzac to Amiens* (1946), C. E. W. Bean is typical in his praise: 'Anzac stood, and still stands, for reckless valour in a good cause, for enterprise, resourcefulness, fidelity, comradeship, and endurance that will never own defeat.'

In purely military terms, however, Pugsley concludes that that the Anzacs were 'over-matched by the objectives they were set, and thrown off balance by unexpectedly difficult terrain and the tenacity of an outnumbered Turkish defence. An amateur force found itself fighting a professional army.' Lieutenant Noel Loutit (10th Battalion) was one of those who reached Third Ridge on the day of the landings. He was, he later admitted, 'a boy sent to do a man's job'.

Those who took part in the landings immediately knew they had participated in something extraordinary. Wilbraham Fowler thought 25 April 1915 'the most historical day in Australian history'. As the first anniversary approached, a group of Australian soldiers training in England sent a letter to Sir Ian Hamilton. It included the words: 'The day draws near that marks

A cemetery on Anzac is pictured on 30 November 1915. The Anzac war dead lie in over 20 cemeteries on the peninsula, both in the beachhead area and at Cape Helles. As they withdrew in December the Anzacs experienced bitter regret at abandoning their dead comrades. (Liddle Collection)

Australia's first birthday. With you on the 25 April last year we laid firmly the foundation of our Military History and in a few days we hope to celebrate a glorious anniversary.' That first anniversary was marked on 25 April 1916 with a service in Westminster Abbey, as well as other commemorations in France and in Australia. 'Anzac day would ever be to Australia what Trafalgar Day was to England,' suggested the prime minister of South Australia. The number and size of spontaneous commemorations in Australia grew apace, and in 1919 Western Australia declared 25 April a public holiday. Under pressure from the Returned Sailors' and Soldiers' Imperial League of Australia, the other states – sometimes hesitantly – followed suit. And in November 1925 the federal government declared the day a national holiday.

Reaction across the Tasman Sea was rather different. The New Zealand Government made 25 April a holiday as early as 1920. Two years later it acceded to pressure from the Returned Services Association to declare the day a full public holiday, with all pubs, hotels and other businesses closed. Yet, by the 1960s, the same association was lobbying for the law to be relaxed to permit its clubrooms to remain open on Anzac Day.

Suzanne Welborn, writing in 1982, emphasizes the particular importance of Anzac identity to Australians. 'Anzac Day means much more to the Australians,' she suggests. 'It was planned and largely fought as Australia's Day. Today in Australia, "Anzac" is another word for "Australian"… Because of this, the war years magnified the Australian legendary image which became personified in the Australian soldier. Australians verified beliefs about themselves on a world stage.' Indeed, the idea of 'mateship', an unquestioning loyalty to one's 'mates', though developed from an idealized image of 19th-century Australian bushmen, has come to distinguish Australian soldiers from all others. It may be argued that such loyalty existed in all armies, but in the post-war period the idea came to symbolize everything about the Australian wartime experience.

New Zealand was a more conservative, even puritanical, country. Unlike Australia, she produced no war literature, other than proud, sombre sections in regimental histories and a single popular history. Some have even proposed that New Zealand should change its national day, commemorating the men of the New Zealand Expeditionary Force on 8 August, when New Zealanders briefly held the summit of Chunuk Bair, rather than 25 April.

While the Gallipoli campaign failed in its military objectives – the capture of Constantinople, and the removal of the Ottoman Empire from the war – the actions and experiences of the Anzac soldiers created an intangible but powerful legacy. The 'Anzac legend' has become an important part of the national identity of both countries, and continues to shape the way its people view both their past and their present.

MUSEUMS AND RE-ENACTMENT

The starting point for anyone who wishes to learn more about the Anzacs must be the Australian War Memorial in Canberra (www.awm.gov.au). The memorial contains a wide range of exhibits covering all aspects of the Anzac experience, as well as an extensive archive and picture library. Smaller military museums in New South Wales, Queensland, South Australia, Tasmania and Western Australia naturally concentrate on the units raised locally since colonization, and all have interesting and varied collections. The museum of the Royal Australian Army Ordnance Corps at Bandiana (Victoria) is